"Each chapter unfolds l[...]
the sanctity of the Ma[...]

A GLIMPSE
―― *of* ――
HEAVEN
ON EARTH

Deacon David Scheuer

DEACON DAVID SCHEUER

foreword by Travis J. Vanden Heuvel, co-author of the bestselling book,
To Heaven & Back: The Journey of a Roman Catholic Priest

A GLIMPSE OF HEAVEN ON EARTH
© David Scheuer. 2023. ALL RIGHTS RESERVED.

Authored by David Scheuer

> Published by Peregrino Press
> Green Bay, WI
> www.peregrino.press

Cover + Interior Design by Peregrino Press
Cover image © Peregrino Press, LLC. ALL RIGHTS RESERVED

No part of this book may be reproduced in any form or by any means, electronic or mechanical, including photocopying, recording, taping, or by any storage and retrieval system, without the written permission of David Scheuer or Peregrino Press.

Publisher's note:
This book, including names, characters, places, and incidents, is based on true events. Some names and identifying details may have been changed for privacy reasons. The author alone bears responsibility for any remaining errors in the text, which are wholly unintentional.

ISBN (hardcover): 978-1-949042-37-5
ISBN (paperback): 978-1-949042-36-8
This title is also available in electronic and audiobook formats.

PUBLISHER'S CATALOGING-IN-PUBLICATION DATA
Scheuer, David
A GLIMPSE OF HEAVEN ON EARTH / Scheuer
1st edition. Green Bay, WI: Peregrino Press, c2023.

Proudly Printed in the United States of America
10 9 8 7 6 5 4 3 2 1

Dedication

To my parents,
the late Frank and Mary Agnes Scheuer:

*The priorities I hold most dear in my life,
a deep faith in God, love for family, and service
to my church and community, have been inspired
by the example Mom and Dad lived in their
lives and passed down to my siblings and me.*

CONTENTS

Acknowledgements	i
A Shared Pilgrimage	v
Introduction	ix
Who I Am	1
Being Called	11
Christian Experience Weekend	23
Meeting Jesus Face to Face	39
The Tornado	51
The Lamb's Supper	61
Bill	71
Forming a New Community	85
Ordination	95
Mother Mary Comes to Me	105
Blessed By Jesus	113
The Blood of Christ	123
Pulling Back the Veil	131
The Weight of the Sins of the World	141
Come Holy Spirit!	153
You've Got to Carry That Weight	161
A Real Pandemic	169
Bringing the Heat	181
More Tears	187
The Holy Spirit is Alive!	195
Corpus Christi	207
Prayer and Fasting	217
A Spiritual Gift	231
Nothing Greater or Holier	239

Acknowledgements

I WISH TO PERSONALLY THANK THE FOLLOWING PEOPLE, who without their inspiration, support, prayers, encouragement, and contributions, this book would not have been written:

Deacon Tim Stevenson for initially planting the seed to write this book.

Mike Reel, my dear friend and brother in Christ, for your love, friendship, and most importantly, for your persistence in not giving up on me. Thank you for introducing me to a relationship with our Blessed Mother through the Rosary, and for inviting me to experience a personal encounter with Jesus Christ and the Holy Spirit that forever changed my life!

The Lakeshore and Denmark Area CEW communities. Your support, prayers, and sacrifices were the catalyst and support that brought me to, and through, diaconate formation, and continue to motivate me in my ministry as a deacon.

My Wednesday morning Adoration/Bible Study Group for your continued love, support, prayers and encouragement that also motivate me in my ministry as a deacon.

Deacons Mike Valenta and Dan Gray, for your support, prayers, spiritual companionship as we walked our faith journeys to the diaconate together in so many ways, and for being dear friends that I can always talk to, lean on, and depend on for support regarding ministry and life.

Karen Valenta, for your friendship, support, and for enthusiastically reading and editing the original version of what would become this book.

Jim Gillis, for motivating me to grow deeper in my faith, and introducing me to what would become a passion for Eucharistic Adoration. Your friendship, support, and holding me spiritually accountable have been huge blessings in my life.

Curt Nelson, for your many prayers, support, help with so many CEW things, and your unfailing friendship.

Monsignor Jim Feely, my spiritual director and mentor, for your prayers, guidance, and for the time spent discussing and discerning what to do regarding the experiences I have had. Your guidance not only led me to share my story through witness talks, but also led me to believe I could actually write a book.

My children, John, and Grace. You will never know how much you have taught me about faith and unconditional love. God uses both of you to speak to me, and is using you to touch and change hearts in people in ways you don't even know. I love you both so much!

My wife Betsy, who I love more than anyone in this world, for asking me to write down the events and dates of my experiences, which began the process of writing this book. Your encouragement, love, support, and taking time to read and edit many versions of what would become this book is more appreciated than you will ever know. For your support of this project, my diaconal ministry, and all of the things that take time away from spending it with you, I am so appreciative. Thank you for supporting me through so many crazy and amazing experiences. God has blessed me with the most amazing wife I could have ever asked for.

FOREWORD
A Shared Pilgrimage

In today's world, where chaos often reigns supreme, our souls yearn for a touchstone of hope. We crave clarity. And divine insight. It was amidst this ever-present search for understanding that I had the honor of serving alongside our author, Deacon David Scheuer, on Bishop Ricken's Diocesan Pastoral Council in the Diocese of Green Bay, Wis. This shared service, a unique convergence of our own spiritual journeys, gave me a front-row seat to the dedication, wisdom, and grace of Deacon Dave. And after exploring *A Glimpse of Heaven on Earth*, I discovered a profound resonance and camaraderie with my brother-in-Christ.

In *A Glimpse of Heaven on Earth*, our friend and author embarks on a deeply personal journey of spiritual exploration and discovery. Motivated by a series of divine encounters and fueled by a passion for sharing his faith, Deacon Dave intertwines vivid accounts of his spiritual experiences with reflections rooted in scripture and Catholic tradition. His writing, beautifully introspective, serves as a bridge between the divine and the everyday, making profound spiritual insights accessible and relatable to all.

With a narrative approach reminiscent of writers like Henri Nouwen and Thomas Merton, the deacon captures the hearts of his readers, inviting us to walk alongside him on a path of faith and wonder. Engaging and earnest, Dave's storytelling captivates; drawing readers into a shared exploration of faith that is both uplifting and transformative. In reading his book, one cannot help but be inspired by his commitment to God and heartened by his unwavering belief in the power of His love.

The journey within these pages is a shared pilgrimage, one where Deacon Dave's encounters with the divine meld seamlessly with the universal truths we, as Catholics, hold dear. From awe-inspiring moments with the Eucharist to the grounding realities of family and service, he offers readers a unique blend of the temporal and the eternal, inviting us to contemplate and strengthen our own spiritual commitments.

The year 2023 marks a time of significant change, especially here in the United States. Divisions have deepened, and spiritual conversations have often become more polarized. In this climate, Deacon Dave's work is balm; gently reminding us of our shared Catholic heritage and the unchanging love of God, providing a grounding presence amidst the maelstrom of modern life.

For the ardent believer, *A Glimpse of Heaven on Earth* reaffirms the cherished tenets of our faith. For those on the periphery, it offers a guiding hand, leading readers through the vast expanse of spiritual wonderment towards the heart of Catholicism and God's love.

In an era marked by uncertainty, Deacon Dave's insights emerge as a beacon of hope. Rooted in Scripture and tradition, his revelations underscore the enduring power of faith, serving as a testament to its transformative influence.

May Deacon's words offer you the comfort, inspiration, and spiritual nourishment that they so naturally foster. Together, let us embark on a pilgrimage of faith; ever reaching for the heavens ... both the one above, and the one here, on Earth.

Travis J. Vanden Heuvel
co-author of the *#1* bestselling book
To Heaven & Back: The Journey of a Roman Catholic Priest

Introduction

Have you ever experienced the presence, power, and fire of the Holy Spirit? A fire so powerful that it led you somewhere you initially did not want to go and fought it as you were being led?

Do you long for the Bread of Life; both being in its presence and in receiving it in the Eucharist? Have you ever had an experience with, or been in the presence of, the Blessed Sacrament that was so powerful and so real that it frightened you, gave you the most amazing sense of peace, and moved you to tears all at the same time? I have experienced all of that ... and more!

Every day, God reveals Himself to us in some way, and some days in multiple ways. Unfortunately, if you are anything like I had been through the first 40 years of my life, you may not have your eyes and your heart open to His presence in your life, open enough to where you recognize God speaking directly to you, revealing Himself to you.

Through God revealing Himself to me, I have come

to realize that there is a very fine, very thin veil between heaven and earth. We cannot pull the veil back ourselves to get a glimpse of heaven here on earth. Only God can do that. I believe that once we open our hearts and minds and allow the Holy Spirit to fully enter in, suddenly those heavenly realities will begin to manifest themselves in our lives. Or to put it more simply, God will begin to pull back the veil, revealing Himself, giving us little glimpses of heaven right here on earth.

As I begin this witness to my own personal experiences of the presence of the Holy Spirit, experiences at Mass and in the presence of the Blessed Sacrament, many of which I have been told are mystical, or supernatural, I feel it is of vital importance to point out that I am not sharing these experiences to make myself look spiritually superior, or holy, or to glorify myself in any way. This witness is solely for the purpose of glorifying God – the Father, Son, and Holy Spirit!

What I am going to share are events that took place over many years, but many of them over a period of approximately six years. These events, or experiences, were so profound they led me to spend five or six months in discernment with my spiritual director, Monsignor (Father) James Feely, a retired diocesan Catholic priest of the Diocese of Green Bay. We prayed about, and discussed these events, trying to figure out why I am having these experiences, and just what it is that God wants me to do with all of this. Through this period of discernment, Father Jim and I concluded that the Holy Spirit was leading me to share what I had been experiencing with others, that this was not something to keep to myself.

This brought about another issue. We weren't sure what would be the best way to go about finding opportunities to witness to what I have experienced. After additional prayerful discernment, Father Jim suggested that I reach out to two people and get their opinion on how to move forward, as they may have connections to people, groups, or organizations that might provide the opportunity to share my story. Those two were Julianne Stanz and Sister Marie Kolbe Zamora OSF, STD.

Julianne Stanz is the director of Parish Life and Evangelization for the Diocese of Green Bay. She is an author, a consultant to the United Sates Conference of Catholic Bishops Committee on Catechesis and Evangelization, as well as being a nationally known speaker. Julianne was also the instructor for my Introduction to Adult and Family Ministry Course during diaconate formation.

Sister Marie Kolbe Zamora was, at that time, the chair of Theology and Ministry at Silver Lake College of the

Holy Family, in Manitowoc, WI, as well as a sought-after speaker at conferences in the Diocese of Green Bay. She since became a faculty member at St. Lawrence Seminary High School in Mount Calvary, WI, and then was appointed to the General Secretariat of the Synod of Bishops at the Vatican.

On August 7, 2019, I emailed them both. I began to email back and forth with both of them, discussing my experiences. It was during an email conversation I had with Sister Marie Kolbe, after I had given her quite a bit of the details of my experiences, that she said to me, "Before you do anything else, you need to discuss this with the bishop. Bishop Ricken needs to know that one of his deacons is having these experiences."

As a result, I reached out to Bishop David Ricken, the bishop of the Diocese of Green Bay, and asked if I could meet with him to discuss the experiences I had been having at Mass and in the presence of the Blessed Sacrament at Eucharistic Adoration. Bishop Ricken and I scheduled a meeting, and on Friday afternoon, August 30, 2019, the bishop and I spent a few hours sitting in the living room of Bishop Ricken's residence, talking one-on-one about what I am going to share with you.

After a lengthy conversation, Bishop Ricken gave me

a book to read and reflect on from his personal library titled, In the Light of the Monstrance, by Saint Peter Julian Eymard, which provided me great insight into the Eucharist. Bishop Ricken also encouraged me to share my experiences with people throughout the Diocese of Green Bay, especially since there has become such a large percentage of Catholics who don't believe in the true presence of Christ in the Eucharist. We discussed a pew survey that had just been issued on Aug. 5, 2019, which stated, "…nearly seven in ten Catholics (69%) say they personally believe that during Catholic Mass, the bread and wine used in Communion "are symbols of the body and blood of Jesus Christ." Just one-third of U.S. Catholics (31%) say they believe that "during Catholic Mass, the bread and wine actually become the body and blood of Jesus."

Since the fall of 2019, I have been regularly going around the Diocese of Green Bay, witnessing to the presence, power, and fire of the Holy Spirit in my life, and to the real presence of Christ in the Eucharist, which has been revealed to me through my experiences.

On Tuesday, August 24, 2021, Deacon Tim Stevenson from St. John-Sacred Heart Parishes in Sherwood and St. John in Wisconsin invited me to come share my witness at Sacred Heart Parish in Sherwood. On Wednesday, October 6, 2021, Deacon Tim invited me back to again share my witness, this time at St. John Parish. I spent quite a bit of time speaking and emailing back and forth with Deacon Tim about my experiences. It was Deacon Tim who first planted the seed to consider writing a book about these experiences.

In the spring of 2022, my wife Betsy asked me if I could write my experiences down, including the dates of when events took place. She told me that she would never remember all of the events and dates but would like them written out, so the information doesn't just get lost or forgotten at some point.

So, Betsy and Deacon Tim were the inspiration for writing about my experiences, with the hope that others could get a glimpse of what I had witnessed. Walk with me now on my journey of experiencing heaven on earth.

Whenever a person turns to the Lord the veil is removed.
(2 Corinthians 3:16)

Who I Am

CHAPTER 1

Who I Am

I WOULD LIKE TO BEGIN BY GIVING SOME BACKGROUND about myself. I married my wife Betsy on June 17, 1989, at St. Mary's Catholic Church in Tisch Mills, WI. We have two grown children, John, and Grace. Betsy and I live in Cooperstown, WI, a small, rural community about 20 miles southeast of Green Bay. I have worked for an architecture firm in Green Bay since March 6, 1984, and was ordained a deacon in the Catholic Church on May 19, 2012.

I grew up in a Catholic family with loving parents. We were somewhat of a typical Catholic family in my hometown of Mishicot, WI. My parents were both products of Catholic grade schools. They came from families of deep faith and that faith was passed on to me and my four brothers and three sisters.

Although I always knew and felt I was loved as a child, my parents never said "I love you" or hugged and kissed us. There just wasn't that kind of affection shown in our home, but as I said, I always knew that my parents loved me.

My parents sent us all to Holy Cross Catholic School in Mishicot for grade school and we all went to four years of religious education during high school. We received our Sacraments – Baptism, First Holy Communion, First Reconciliation, and Confirmation – at Holy Cross Parish. Missing Sunday Mass, or Mass on Holy Days of Obligation, was never an option. If we went somewhere for a weekend – camping with relatives or friends, or a to a friend's cottage, it didn't matter – we were expected to make it to Sunday Mass, wherever we were. My mom would also ask us to bring home a bulletin as proof that we attended Sunday Mass. We used to refer to that bulletin as our receipt.

We were expected to go to confession regularly, and were taken by my parents to the Parish Reconciliation Services held each year during Advent and Lent. As a family, we also attended Stations of the Cross every Sunday each year during Lent. Praying before meals was just part of what we did as a family – even if we were eating in a restaurant. Boy was that embarrassing! My brothers and I were all Mass servers growing up. Two of my sisters sang in the church choir, and one of my brothers, two of my sisters and I were lectors for Mass throughout our high school years.

My dad, Frank Scheuer, was the parish maintenance man from the time I began fifth grade until I was out of college. This meant that my brothers and I were expected to help my dad with setting up for parish events, as well as taking down and cleaning up after parish events. We were dragged out of bed at 4 a.m. on winter mornings when it had snowed overnight to get the sidewalks and driveways around the church and school shoveled before teachers and students arrived for school and we helped mow the lawn of the parish grounds and cemetery during the summer. As a matter of fact, my summer job throughout my years of college was working with my dad, cleaning the school, painting classrooms, stripping and waxing floors of the school – basically getting the building ready for the upcoming school year as well as weekly cleaning of the church.

My mom, Mary Agnes (Haen) Scheuer, was a teacher at Mishicot High School. She also taught religious education at our parish. At one point or another, Mom was a member of nearly every committee or board in our parish and was also likely the chairperson for those committees at some point when I was growing up. She was also active in the Green Bay Diocesan Council of Catholic Women, which she also chaired.

In February of 2013, my mom shared with my sister

Marie and me that she had what I would describe as a mystical experience during Mass when she was a freshman in high school. My mom attended high school in East De Pere, WI, about 15 miles north of Greenleaf, the town her family lived in. Because the high school was in a different school district than the one my mom's family lived in, my grandpa would drive my mom into town for school on his way to work every morning. He would drop her off about 1½ hours before school began. There was a Catholic Church a few blocks from the high school my mom attended, and she would walk over and attend morning Mass each day as a way to pass the time before school began.

My mom explained to us that one morning at Mass, as the priest was praying the Eucharistic prayer and held up the host at the consecration, the priest physically changed in appearance. She said his appearance physically changed into Jesus Christ before her eyes.

At the time she told us about this, I was 50 years old, so I asked my mom why she had never shared this story with us before. Her response was that she always felt it was something special that was just between her and Jesus. She stated this in a kind of matter-of-fact way, almost as if it wasn't that big of a deal! I told her that it was a big deal, and that it is something she should be sharing with people. I said that her family certainly needs to know about this, as it may help them to believe in Christ's true presence in the Eucharist more fully! She just seemed to shrug it off.

My parents were also the local 4-H Club Leaders and my dad spent time as a village board trustee. As you can see, service to their church and community were everyday parts of my parent's lives. Service to others was modeled to me by my parents throughout my formative years and beyond.

Although my upbringing very much revolved around the church, and focused on service, the truth is, for the first 40 years of my life I just kind of went through the motions of my faith. Looking back, I believe part of the reason for that is that I wasn't very well catechized. I grew up in the 1960s and 1970s, post Second Vatican Council, and it seems like those who were teaching me about the faith were almost stumbling their way through, trying to figure out how to teach the faith with all the changes that were coming out of the Second Vatican Council. As a result, a lot of the things that my parents had learned about the Catholic faith in their catechism classes were not being taught to my generation. Many of the Church's beautiful prayers and devotions, in particular, devotions to the Blessed Virgin Mary, like the Rosary, were not taught. Other things like Eucharistic Adoration were never experienced during my youth. As a matter of fact, the first time

I ever experienced Eucharistic Adoration I was in my early 40s. This was something completely new to me!

Looking back, I now realize that there was something missing in my life. There was a nagging feeling that there was something more, but I was not sure what that something was. I spent way too much of my life longing for things that I didn't realize I was missing because they were things I had never experienced before. All that would dramatically begin to change, through one amazing encounter with the Holy Spirit!

Take to heart these words which I command you today. Keep repeating them to your children. Recite them when you are at home and when you are away, when you lie down and when you get up.
(Deuteronomy 6:6-7)

Reflection questions:

How has your family and upbringing shaped your faith life and your relationship with God?

How has your relationship with God changed throughout the years of your life?

Prayer:

Lord Jesus Christ,

Help me to be a witness of truth and faith to all my loved ones. May I pass on my faith and trust in you through the example of my words and actions. Reveal yourself to my family and friends, and may your grace fill their hearts in such a way that they know and trust in you.

Amen.

Being Called

CHAPTER 2

Being Called

To fully understand some of my experiences, and how they are interrelated, I would like to share my call to the diaconate. My call was very different from the men I went through diaconate formation with. Some of the men had attended seminary either in high school, or in college, but realized they weren't being called to the priesthood. Years later, they entered the diocesan diaconate formation program. Others had their parish priest or parishioners tell them they thought they would make a good deacon and should consider looking into diaconate formation. My call was very different from those experiences. Nobody ever told me I would make a good deacon!

When I first began to get my call to the diaconate, I did not even belong to a parish. In the spring of 1991, almost two years after getting married, Betsy and I moved from my hometown of Mishicot, WI, to Green Bay, WI, since we both had jobs in Green Bay. When we moved to Green Bay, we didn't join a parish. We lived about 2½ blocks from St. Bernard's Catholic Church on the east side of Green Bay, but for some reason we didn't feel it was that important to actually join the parish. I was still praying, and we were going to Mass on Sundays – well, at least most Sundays – but I was the least active in my faith that I have been in my entire life. I was basically just going through the motions as far as my faith life was concerned, doing what I thought was the bare minimum, (little did I know God expected much more from me). Yet it was in the context of this that God first called me to the diaconate.

At the time, one of my very dear friends, Mike Reel, began to have a deep devotion to the Blessed Virgin Mary. His in-laws had taken a trip to Medjugorje in southwestern Bosnia and Herzegovina, where the Virgin Mary has been appearing since 1981 and giving messages for the world. While there, they had a very spiritually profound experience. As a result, they began to encourage my friend Mike and his wife Mary Kay to make it a priority in their lives to have a devotion to the Virgin Mary. They also encouraged them to begin praying the Rosary.

Mike is a home builder/carpenter by trade and I remember being at his house one Saturday afternoon, helping him pour concrete for an addition he was putting onto his house. He and his wife began talking about the Virgin Mary and how important having a devotion to Her was for them. They began encouraging me to start praying the Rosary and making the Blessed Mother an important part of my life.

At the time I was 30 years old and had never been taught how to pray the Rosary. As a matter of fact, I didn't even own a Rosary. My parents never taught me to pray the Rosary. I had attended a Catholic grade school, attended religious education classes at my parish during high school, and attended a Catholic college, but had never been taught to pray the Rosary. It was something that I never remember even being brought up at home or in any religion classes I had throughout all of those years of school.

Mike explained that praying the Rosary was very simple. You pray an Our Father, and then ten Hail Marys, and you repeat it five times. So, I began praying the Rosary – on my fingers – simply praying an Our Father, and then 10 Hail Marys, and I repeated it five times. Mike and Mary Kay never mentioned anything about praying the Glory Be, the Fatima Prayer, or any of the mysteries of the Rosary. So, my version of praying the Rosary was simply praying an Our Father, and then 10 Hail Marys, and I repeated it five times.

At this same time, I was both working for the architecture firm in Green Bay and coaching the boys' varsity basketball team at my alma mater, Mishicot High School. After work each day, I would drive from Green Bay to

Mishicot for practice and drive back home to Green Bay after practice. It was about a 40-minute drive each way.

I thought my life was going perfectly, heading in the direction I had planned. I was working in a profession that I had dreamed of since I was in about fifth grade. I'm certain, looking back, that God put that desire for architecture in my heart for a reason, as yet another dream surfaced. As a senior in high school, I changed my mind about what I wanted to do for a career. As a result, I initially went to college to be a physical education teacher, which I figured would also give me an opportunity to coach high school sports. After a year of college, that plan changed back to architecture, but the physical education and coaching theory classes I had taken during that initial year of college opened doors for me to begin coaching basketball. As I had success coaching, I began to dream about eventually coaching basketball as a profession at the college level. As I said, it seemed like everything was going according to my plans. And then the unexpected happened.

I don't remember the exact date, but I'm quite certain it was during the winter of 1993 when I first received my call to the diaconate. The one thing I do remember is that I know exactly where I was when it happened. On that winter evening in 1993, as I was driving alone in the car back to Green Bay after basketball practice in Mishicot,

I was on Interstate 43, about 2 miles north of Denmark, WI, when something happened that would change my life forever.

I was praying the Rosary, and counting the prayers on my fingers, since I still did not own a Rosary at that time. Suddenly, I heard an audible voice, an actual voice, that said to me, "Dave, I want you to be a deacon," and it scared the heck out of me! I had my life all planned out and everything seemed to be going according to my plans. This did not fit into them! There is the old saying, "If you want to make God laugh, tell him what your plans are"! That's kind of the situation I was in.

At the time, I really didn't know what a deacon was, and I didn't know what a deacon did. All I knew for sure was that I did not want to be one! I remember thinking at the time that I couldn't tell anyone about hearing a voice because they would think I was crazy. So, instead, I decided I was just going to try to ignore it. But the more I tried to ignore that voice, the louder the voice was coming through. I literally tried to ignore God's call for nearly 10 years, but God was persistent.

As time went on and I tried to ignore this voice that continued to tell me, "I want you to be a deacon," it was actually driving me crazy! It got to the point after about two years, that I finally decided to say something to my wife.

One evening when I got home from work, I told Betsy that I had been hearing this voice that was telling me, "I want you to become a deacon." Of course, she thought I was crazy! I remember her asking, rather puzzled, "You're hearing a voice?!?" All I could tell her was, "Yes, and I've been hearing it for a while." Betsy then said something that, in hindsight, was very profound, but it didn't seem that way at the time. She said to me, "Maybe God doesn't want you to become a deacon right now. Maybe he just wants you to get active in the church again and see where it leads."

At that moment in time, after mustering up enough courage to actually tell her about this voice, it seemed to me that she wasn't being very supportive – or at least not providing the support I thought I needed at that time – so I decided to continue to ignore the voice, and I continued trying to ignore it for another eight years.

On March 3, 1995, not long after I had told Betsy about hearing "the voice," the grandfather of a close friend, Mike Valenta, passed away. I had spent a little bit of time with Mike's grandfather. I had played cards with him, Mike, and a few of our friends on a couple of occasions, but I remember very vividly when Mike told me his grandfather had died, because it was such a profoundly beautiful story that moved me deeply.

Mike mentioned to me that his grandfather had been ill, and someone from his church came to his grandfather's home to visit and bring him communion. Immediately after his grandfather received communion, he closed his eyes and peacefully passed away. At the time, I was so moved by hearing how his grandfather died, and I still am! I remember thinking to myself at that time, "If I could choose the perfect and most beautiful way to die, that would be it – receive Jesus in the Eucharist, and peacefully pass away." As a Catholic, shouldn't that be our ultimate desire for when our time on this earth comes to an end? For that reason, the story of Mike's grandfather's death has remained with me all these years.

In November of 1995, we found out that Betsy was pregnant with our first child. One of the first things we began talking about during Betsy's pregnancy was that we would need to get our baby baptized once the baby was born, which meant we needed to join a church. In May of 1996, we went over to St. Bernard's Catholic Church in Green Bay and registered as new parish members. It only took us five years to register as parish members!

On July 9, 1996, our son John was born. I never realized until the moment of his birth that I could instantly love someone so completely, even though I had just seen him for the very first time. I did not know that kind of unconditional love could exist and exist so immediately. I began to have a better understanding of God's unconditional love for us as our Father.

On Sunday, August 4, 1996, our son was baptized at St. Bernard's. The parish celebrated the Sacrament of Baptism during the afternoon on the first Sunday of each month, and there were five other children baptized at the same Baptismal Rite as John. One of the things that really surprised me about John's baptism was that the parish had a deacon, Deacon John Laurent, doing the baptisms. I didn't know that a deacon could perform a baptism. Initially I thought, "Is this a valid baptism if a priest doesn't do it?" It just goes to show how little I actually knew about valid Sacraments in the Catholic Church. I also remember thinking at the time, "If this is actually valid, being able to do baptisms as a deacon would really be cool! Maybe this deacon thing wouldn't be that bad."

God saved us and called us to a holy life, not according to our works but according to his own design and the grace bestowed on us in Christ Jesus before time began.
(2 Timothy 1:9)

Reflection questions:

Do you spend silent time alone with God listening, allowing your heart to be open to hearing his voice speak to you?

God is calling each of us to a holy life. To what might God be calling you in this season of your life?

Prayer:

God, help me to listen. Help me to listen deeply, from the very depths of my soul, so that I may hear your voice speaking to me. Teach me to distinguish the difference between the noise of this world and your voice speaking to my heart. I know that you speak to me every day. Today, help me to truly listen, and hear your voice.

Amen.

Christian Experience Weekend

CHAPTER 3

Christian Experience Weekend

In February 1998, my friend Mike Reel, the same friend who encouraged me to begin praying the Rosary and begin a devotion to the Virgin Mary, attended a retreat in Manitowoc, WI, called a Christian Experience Weekend retreat, also known as CEW.

Christian Experience Weekend is an adaptation of a Cursillo retreat. It was developed in the Diocese of Dubuque, Iowa, as a two-day alternate renewal program that begins on Friday evening and runs through late Sunday afternoon – rather than the Thursday evening until late Sunday evening format of Cursillo – which they found to be more conducive to most people's schedules.

After having attended his first Christian Experience Weekend retreat, Mike began inviting me to attend a CEW. Mike invited me to the Men's Christian Experience Weekend for four straight years, and each time he invited me, I made up excuses for not being able to go, but the truth is, at that point in life, I really did not want to "waste" an entire weekend hanging out with a bunch of "Jesus Freaks." Little did I know that I would eventually become one of those "Jesus Freaks."

In December of 1997, Betsy, John, and I moved into a new home we had built in the rural Denmark, WI, area to be closer to both of our parents, so John could spend more time with his grandparents. Our home was now about 10 to 15 minutes away from both of our parents' homes. The biggest difference about moving into our new home this time, was that we immediately became members of St. James Catholic Church in Cooperstown, just over a mile away from our home.

In February of 2000, we found out that Betsy was pregnant again. On October 10, 2000, our daughter Grace was born. In the hospital, immediately after Grace's birth, the nurse asked me what name we had chosen for our daughter. I was so moved by emotion, that same instantaneous feeling of unconditional love I had felt at John's birth, that I was literally sobbing. I couldn't even answer her, and Betsy had to answer instead. It was truly a moment of grace in my life!

On Sunday, November 26, 2000, our beautiful daughter Grace was baptized by Father Ron Colombo at St. James Catholic Church in Cooperstown.

On the evening of Sunday, April 21, 2002, I received a phone call from my younger brother Joe. He told me that my dad had been rushed by ambulance to Holy Family Memorial Hospital in Manitowoc, WI, after complaining about chest pains. We loaded the kids up in the car and quickly drove down to the hospital. When we arrived, most of my family was there, all but my oldest brother and his wife, and my youngest sister, her husband and daughter, as both siblings live about 2½ hours away.

We stood by in the waiting room while the medical professionals were running my dad through a bunch of tests. After about a 45-minute wait, the doctor came out and told us that my dad was not having a heart attack, but was still complaining about chest pain, so the doctor decided to keep my dad in the hospital overnight for observation.

Before leaving the hospital that evening, each of my siblings and their families went into the room my dad would be staying in overnight to say goodnight. Betsy, John, Grace, and I went in for a short visit, and as we were about to leave, I walked over to the bed, leaned over, and gave my dad a hug and said, "I love you Dad." As we were walking out to our car, it struck me that I had never told my dad that I loved him before this and I couldn't ever remember having hugged him either.

That night, just after midnight, the telephone rang, waking me out of a deep sleep. It was my mom, and she told me that my dad had just died. She told me that he had suffered an aneurysm in the main artery into his heart and went very suddenly.

As I laid there in bed, in shock and crying, all I could think about was that the first time I ever told my dad I loved him was the last thing I ever said to him. I spent quite a bit of time over the next month or two playing that back in my mind and feeling really guilty. This was the man I had loved the most in my life. I had 40 years to tell my dad I loved him and I came so close to never having said it!

I made a commitment shortly after my dad's death to make sure I tell those I love just how I feel about them, so that I never have to live with the regret of never having said "I love you."

A few days after my dad had died, I was having a conversation with our parish priest, Father Ron Colombo. He told me how sorry he was about my dad's passing and that he was praying for me and my entire family. He then said something that I won't ever forget. Father Ron said to me, "Remember that there are a lot of people praying for you right now. Friends, family, parish members, they are all there to lift you up in prayer, to carry you, to be a shoulder to cry on, and to support you in whatever way you need. But never forget, the most important person who is walking this journey with you is Jesus. Walk with Him, lean on Him, pray to Him, cry with Him. That's what He is there for. He understands your pain and grief more than anyone."

Well, over the next few months, I walked that journey with Jesus. I prayed to Jesus, I leaned on Jesus, and I cried with Jesus. The experience of my dad's death led me to spend a great deal of time praying, as I was trying to sort everything out. Much of that sorting out was asking Jesus to help me through my feelings of guilt. But what I didn't realize was really happening is that my relationship with Jesus was growing stronger because of that time spent in prayer.

During the summer of 2002, we decided to enroll John in first grade at All Saints Catholic School in Denmark. After quite a bit of discussion, we decided that since John would be attending school at All Saints, it made sense for us to join the parish where John would be attending school. After being members at St. James Parish in Cooperstown for just over four years, we were changing parishes.

Four years after being initially invited to attend a

Christian Experience Weekend retreat, and about eight months after my dad's death, Mike Reel again invited me to attend the upcoming retreat. This time, he did not verbally invite me. Instead, he sent me a handwritten letter in the mail, which said that he was going to be leading the upcoming retreat as the lay rector and he asked me if I would attend to support him as this was going to be a huge step for him in his faith journey. Mike is a friend who has always been there to support me in so many ways and his handwritten letter guilted me into feeling that I needed to attend, if for no other reason than to support him. Maybe all that time praying after my dad's death had somehow softened my heart a little bit to make it easier to say, "yes," but even with that, deep down inside, I really did not want to go.

On the evening of Friday, February 14, 2003, Betsy had to push me out the door to get me to go to CEW. When I arrived in Manitowoc, I parked my truck. I walked into what was known as the Life Teen House at Holy Innocents Catholic Parish in Manitowoc, WI, with a rock-hard heart, to attend a retreat that I really didn't want to be at. As I looked around the room after arriving, I was shocked to see two other friends of both Mike and me who were also there, Mike Valenta (now Deacon Mike), and Steve Rasmussen. Mike had sent each of them a similar handwritten letter to the one he had sent to me. The amazing thing is that none of us knew the other two would be attending. Saturday of the retreat weekend, February 15, 2003, was my dad's birthday. It was his first birthday since his death and I spent quite a bit of time that day thinking about my dad.

During a Christian Experience Weekend retreat, as a group you pray the Prayer to the Holy Spirit 10 different times. As the retreat began, I was just reading the words to that prayer, just saying them, not really praying them, mostly because I came with somewhat of a bad attitude and a very closed heart. But something happened on that Saturday that I never could have anticipated. I actually started to pray the words of The Prayer to the Holy Spirit, and as I started praying those words, "Come Holy Spirit, fill the hearts of your faithful and enkindle in them the fire of your love," something that was life changing happened to me! Suddenly while praying those words, my rock-hard heart began to crack open just a tiny little bit, and the presence, power, and fire of the Holy Spirit came gushing in and filled my heart to overflowing!! It was like nothing I had ever experienced before, and so difficult to put into actual words! It was frightening, exhilarating, extremely peaceful, and able to move me to tears all at the same time! It was a feeling I didn't ever want to lose!

I didn't realize it at the time, but from that moment

on, my life would never be the same! When Sunday afternoon came and the retreat came to a close, I did not want to leave! This retreat that I really didn't want to be at on Friday evening was now something I did not want to end!

If you have never had a Holy Spirit moment, a personal encounter with our Lord, I pray that you too can have that experience of having your heart set on fire by the Holy Spirit. It is one of the most amazing feelings I have ever experienced and it is truly life changing!

When I got home on Sunday evening and walked through the door, the very first thing I said to Betsy was, "I need to go talk to Father Ron about becoming a deacon." The next Sunday after Mass, I waited outside the church as Father Ron greeted people as they left church, until no one else was around. I hate to admit it, but I was a bit embarrassed and didn't want anyone to hear what I was about to discuss with Father Ron. I then told him that I felt like I was being called by God to be a deacon. Father Ron was amazing! He invited me over to the rectory on Tuesday evening to discuss it. After spending about two hours talking with Father, he believed I really was being called by God. He set up an appointment for Betsy and me for the following Tuesday with Deacon Paul Grimm, the diaconate formation director for the Diocese of Green Bay.

The following Tuesday, we met with Deacon Paul at the diocesan offices in Green Bay, and after a fairly lengthy conversation, Deacon Paul told me that I could fill out the application for diaconate formation if I would like, but he also said that he was certain that I would not be accepted. He told us that the diaconate is a ministry of service, and I had no track record of service as an adult in the church. It brought me right back to what Betsy had said to me when I initially told her about hearing "the voice," that maybe God wasn't calling me to be a deacon right now, maybe he just wants me to get active in the church and see where it leads. Yes, Betsy was right…and sometimes it's hard for me as a husband to admit that my wife was right and I was wrong!

I went home following that meeting and jumped in with both feet. I began volunteering and became very active in our parish. I volunteered to be a religious education teacher, to be a lector, an usher. I became a member of the Parish Total Board of Education, which I also chaired. I became a member of the school's marketing committee. I volunteered to be part of a three-person youth minister team as we began a youth ministry program with four linked parishes. I also became very active in Christian Experience Weekend retreats.

I found that as I began lectoring and spending more

time with the scriptures in preparation for reading at Mass, my desire to dig deeper into the Word of God began to grow. As I began teaching religious education, I found I was learning right along with the students I was teaching and my desire to learn more about my Catholic faith was growing. As I began my role as a co-youth minister, the enthusiasm of the high school students who participated in youth ministry was rubbing off on me. As I began participating in jail ministry, I began to be much more compassionate to those who find themselves in less-than-ideal circumstances. As I was asked to give witness talks at Christian Experience Weekend retreats, I found that I had a desire to share my faith journey and experiences with others. It felt as though God placed me right where he needed me.

As I was getting actively involved in our parish, the one thing I really desired to do was share the Holy Spirit experience I had had at that Christian Experience Weekend retreat with everyone I knew. I wanted everyone to be able to experience what I had experienced, and the one person I wanted to share that experience with more than anyone else was Betsy.

I began inviting Betsy to attend the women's Christian Experience Weekend retreat, but just like me, she made excuses not to go. Even though she had recognized the amazing impact that this had had on me, how it had been life changing for me, it wasn't enough to convince her to attend.

Many of our friends, both husbands and wives, were beginning to attend and were getting very actively involved with the Christian Experience Weekend retreat community. As I got more and more involved over the next few years, Betsy made it pretty clear she wasn't ready to attend because she didn't want to spend a weekend away from our children. Yet I continued to invite her each time there was another women's retreat scheduled.

I had invited Betsy to three consecutive women's retreats and each time she declined my invitation. As the fourth women's Christian Experience Weekend retreat after my having attended my first retreat, was fast approaching, I again began inviting Betsy to attend. She again said no, she didn't want to attend, but I continued to bug her about it.

On Wednesday evening, Nov. 2, 2005, we were at the kitchen table, eating supper with our children and I asked Betsy again if she would go on the retreat. She responded by telling me, "I already told you I'm not going to go. Please don't ask me again." But, because I'm a guy, and apparently have a thick head and don't know any better, I immediately asked her again! She got upset with me and said, "I told you I'm not going! If you ask me again, I'm never going to go!"

My son John was in third grade at the time and was sitting directly across the table from Betsy. He looked at her and asked, "Mom, do you love Jesus?" Betsy replied, "Of course I love Jesus." To which John replied, "If you love Him, you will go!" I was shocked, yet amazed by John's words. I looked over at Betsy, and she had tears running down her cheeks. She looked over at me and said, "I guess I'm going on a retreat!" As Psalm 8 says, "Through the mouths of children and babes…"

On Friday evening, November 11, 2005, the kids and I dropped Betsy off at the Life Teen House at what is now known as St. Francis of Assisi Parish in Manitowoc for her first Christian Experience Weekend retreat. I'm not sure what all happened on that weekend retreat for Betsy, but based on her reaction when she came home, it was evident that she too had an encounter with the Holy Spirit similar to mine. The first thing she said to me when she got home was, "We need to start that deacon thing right away!"

The very next day, I called Deacon Paul Grimm, the diaconate formation director, and set up a meeting for Betsy and me for the following day. Within two days of Betsy returning from her retreat, we were beginning the application process to my becoming a deacon in the Catholic Church! I was accepted into diaconate formation in July 2006, and began my diaconate aspirancy year in September 2006.

> *"But you will receive power when the Holy Spirit comes upon you, and you will be my witnesses in Jerusalem, throughout Judea and Samaria, and to the ends of the earth."*
> *(Acts 1:8)*

Reflection questions:

> Jesus promised he would send us the Holy Spirit. How and when have you experienced the Holy Spirit in your life?
>
> Who has been a witness to Christ to you in your life?

Prayer:

> Holy Spirit, I ask you to enter into my heart and abide in me. May your presence, living within me, set my heart on fire with the fire of your love.
>
> Amen.

Meeting Jesus Face to Face

CHAPTER 4

Meeting Jesus Face to Face

I HAVE HAD GOD SPEAK TO ME IN MANY WAYS AND THROUGH many people in my life. He has spoken to me though my children, through friends, through priests, deacons and religious. He has also spoken to me through people I have met on a single occasion in my life. Some I don't even know their names.

On the weekend of February 17-19, 2006, God spoke to me through four individuals, three of whom I had never met prior to that weekend and have never seen since.

On Thursday, February 16, 2006, we had a pretty significant snowstorm in Northeastern Wisconsin. It was officially classified as a blizzard. We saw 13 to 15 inches of snow fall throughout the region, with winds up to 40 mph winds that continued throughout the following day.

On the evening of Friday, February 17, the annual men's Christian Experience Weekend retreat was to take place in Manitowoc, and I was asked to be part of the team that was putting on the retreat. My role was to be part of a three-man team that planned all the prayer services, a reconciliation service, and the Liturgies for the retreat.

Friday morning after snow-blowing out my driveway, I drove to work in Green Bay, about 20 miles northwest of my home. Luckily, I had a 4-wheel drive pickup truck since the roads were drifting badly. That afternoon, I had to leave work early so I could stop at home and pick up the things I needed for the retreat, and to be able to arrive at the retreat by 5 p.m. I needed to be there early to help get things prepared for the Team Liturgy that begins at 5:30 p.m. Immediately following the Liturgy, the team has supper together before the weekend retreatants begin arriving at 7 p.m.

I arrived home from work a bit later than I had planned due to bad road conditions. I quickly grabbed the things I needed for the retreat, threw them in my truck, and started driving to Manitowoc, which is about a 20-mile drive to the southeast of my home. I started out taking a back road, rather than the highway, because it's about a five-mile shorter drive. I got about a quarter mile from my house and the road was pretty badly drifted when I realized that I had left a bag at home that had Liturgy and prayer service documents in it, so I turned around in a driveway and headed back home.

Once I got home and grabbed the bag I had forgotten, I decided it might be a good idea to take the highway down to Manitowoc, since the wind was still blowing very hard and the one back road I drove on was pretty badly drifted. With my truck still in 4-wheel drive, I headed out to the highway, about a one-mile drive from my house.

I got onto the highway and started driving south, and within a half mile, I noticed there was a car pulled over on the righthand side of the road (also headed south) with its hazard lights flashing. The car had apparently been there for a while because the entire passenger side of the car was buried by a snow drift. There was no way that you would have been able to get the passenger side doors of the car open because the snow had drifted so heavily against them.

As I was driving past the car, a hand suddenly stuck out of the window on the driver's side door and began waving. I am ashamed to say that I continued to drive past. My thought at the moment was, "I'm going to be late getting to the retreat. I can't stop!" I got about a half-mile down the road and my conscience got the best of me. I remember thinking to myself, "Dave, you're heading to a retreat to help people develop a deeper relationship with Christ, and you can't stop and help this person!" I turned around in the next driveway and went back to see if I could be of any help.

I drove back past the car and turned around again and pulled up directly behind the car. I got out of my truck and walked up to the car. As I walked up, the window opened again, and an elderly lady stuck her head out of the window. I noticed there was also an elderly man in the front passenger side seat. The lady told me that every Friday afternoon she would drive her friend, who was in the front seat with her, to the grocery store in Denmark, about five miles north of where we were, because he couldn't drive. On their way home, the car started running rough and eventually just died on them. She also told me that she had called the county sheriff's department, and was told an officer would be right there, but it had been about 45 minutes that they had been sitting there and they were both freezing. I asked them if they would like to come sit in my warm truck and wait for the officer and they were both very happy to be able to get into my warm vehicle.

As we sat in my truck and talked, I felt so sorry for the both of them. They were both shivering, and their noses were running, but they were very happy and appreciative to be sitting inside in the warmth of my truck. After about 20 minutes of waiting, and still no police officer having shown up, I asked them if I could load up their groceries in my truck and drive them home. The lady immediately said with a big smile on her face, "Yes, thank you!"

I went to the car and got all the groceries out and put them in my truck. I then drove them about five to six miles down the road to the elderly gentleman's house. I helped both of them into the house and then went out and brought all the bags of groceries up to the door and handed them to the lady inside. After I brought the last bag of groceries to the door and handed them to the woman, she reached over, grabbed me by the forearm, looked me square in the eye and said, "God bless you!"

As I hopped back into my truck and continued my journey to the retreat in Manitowoc, I was feeling really guilty about the fact that I nearly drove past those two people and left them sitting there freezing. I arrived at the retreat site just in time for the beginning of the Team Liturgy, and although I was trying to concentrate on the Mass, I still had this nagging feeling of guilt, which continued throughout that evening and the next day.

As part of the retreat experience, we had a reconciliation service on Saturday evening. There were four or five priests at the reconciliation service to hear confessions that evening. I went to confession to Father Dan Dewane that evening. He was priest who had been born and raised in Manitowoc and when he retired, he moved back to his hometown.

After confessing my sins, I told Father Dan that I had something that was really nagging at my conscience. He asked what the problem was and I told him about my experience the previous afternoon and how guilty I felt about having almost left the two elderly people sitting in their car as I drove past them. Father Dan looked at me and said, "Ultimately, you did the right thing, you did go back, so there was no sin committed that needed to be confessed, so you really don't need to feel guilty."

Then he said to me, "I would like to tell you a story," and he told me a story about his mother and his childhood. He said that when he was growing up, his mother would always tell him and his siblings that when they knew that they were supposed to do something, but they didn't want to do it because it was too difficult, or it was just way out of their comfort zone, that those were the times that you absolutely needed to show up and do that particular thing. She told them that those are the moments in your life that you get to meet Jesus face to face.

He then told me, "I wasn't feeling very good this evening after supper and I decided that I would just stay home and wasn't going to come here tonight to hear confessions." He then said, "Then my mother's words from my childhood began running though my head, and I thought to myself, maybe this is my opportunity to meet Jesus face to face. Once I started thinking about it that way, there was no way that I wasn't showing up tonight! I don't want to miss an opportunity to meet Jesus face to face!"

I don't know if I was the face of Jesus for Father Dan that evening, or if one of the other guys who went to confession to him that evening was, but I do know this... Father Dan was definitely the face of Christ for me that evening!

Sunday evening after the retreat had concluded, I drove home taking the back roads rather than the highway. When I got a little over a mile away from my house, believe it or not, I noticed that there was a car pulled over on the side of the road with its hazard lights flashing! This time, I didn't drive past. I pulled over right away!

As I walked up to the driver's side door, a young man stuck his head out the window and thanked me for stopping. He then told me that he was a college student who had gone home for the weekend and was now on his way back to school and that he had gotten a flat tire. He told me that the problem was he didn't have a cell phone to call his parents to come help him and his spare tire was sitting in his parents' garage. He then asked me if I would be able to drive him back to his parents' house. He said he could have his dad bring him back with his truck and help him change the tire. He really just needed a ride back home. I didn't hesitate to agree to giving him a ride back home.

So, the young man hopped up into my truck and I turned around and went back a number of miles in the direction I had just come from. When we got to his parents' house, I pulled up in the driveway in front of the garage. As he began climbing out of the truck, he suddenly stopped, reached over, grabbed me by the forearm, looked me square in the eye and said, "God bless you!"

As the young man did and said the exact same thing as the woman had done on Friday evening, I felt a chill run up my spine. I had a very powerful feeling that I had been looking directly into the face of Christ on three separate occasions that weekend!

"Amen, I say to you, whatever you did for one of these least brothers of mine, you did for me." (Matthew 25:40)

Reflection questions:

When we serve those in need, we in turn serve Christ. How have you served someone in need and in turn experienced the face of Christ?

Who in your life has been of service to you at your time of need, where you in turn were potentially the face of Christ for them?

Prayer:

Dearest Lord, I ask that you fill me with your grace, so that in every person I meet and speak with today, I am able to see and recognize Your Face in them. I ask this through Your Holy Name.

Amen!

The Tornado

CHAPTER 5

The Tornado

As most parents have probably experienced, taking a young child to Mass almost seemed like a waste of time. That was the case with my son John. Betsy and I didn't really get much out of the Mass because we were so distracted by always trying to get John to settle down or keep him occupied during Mass.

By the time John got to be two years old, it got even worse, as he was also talking during Mass and was escaping the pew and running up the aisle toward the altar. Numerous times, I had to go and chase John up the aisle, grab him, and bring him back to our pew.

Betsy and I struggled to find anything that worked to keep him quiet or settled down. Like many other parents, we brought big Ziploc bags full of Cheerios to Mass. We brought a stack of books, a bunch of Hot Wheels cars for him to play with – you name it. We tried just about everything to keep him occupied.

One Sunday, when John was about 2½ years old, as we knelt down at the beginning of the Eucharistic Prayer,

I had John sit on the top of the back rest of the pew in front of me with his legs hanging over the front side of the backrest of the pew. His back was tight against my chest, so that we were cheek to cheek. I held him tightly in a bear hug so he couldn't squirm away.

As Father Ron was praying the prayers of consecration and raised the Host, I whispered in John's ear, "Jesus is in the bread." When Father Ron raised the chalice, I whispered in John's ear, "Jesus is in the cup." What happened next was amazing! John's total attention went straight to the altar, and he completely settled down! He remained settled down and his full attention was on the altar for the rest of Mass! I remember thinking, "That was pretty cool," so Betsy and I decided to try the same thing the following week at Mass to see what would happen.

The next Sunday at Mass, as the Eucharistic Prayer began, and we knelt down, I again held John tightly as he sat on the top of the back rest of the pew in front of me with his back tight against my chest. We again were cheek to cheek.

At the consecration, as Father Ron raised the Host, I once again whispered in John's ear, "Jesus is in the bread." As Father Ron raised the chalice, I once again whispered in John's ear, "Jesus is in the cup." Just like the week before,

John completely settled down, and his full attention was on the altar for the rest of Mass.

We continued to do this week after week, month after month, and it always produced the exact same results. After maybe a month or two of this same scenario, one Sunday at Mass, as I whispered in John's ear, "Jesus is in the bread... Jesus is in the cup," John whispered back, "Daddy, do you see the tornado?" My response was, "No, I don't see any tornado. Where do you see a tornado?" John immediately pointed up toward the altar. I wanted to know what he was seeing!

This same verbal exchange continued for weeks. Every week at Mass when I whispered, "Jesus is in the bread... Jesus is in the cup," John would ask me if I could see the tornado. Betsy and I were becoming very curious about what it was he thought he was seeing.

Finally, one Sunday after Mass when Betsy and I were buckling John into his car seat in the car out in the parking lot, we asked him what the tornado looked like that he saw during Mass? In a very matter-of-fact manner, he said, while making a circular motion with his finger, "It's the angels coming down from the ceiling." His response gave me chills! All I could think was, "Wow! I want to see that tornado!"

John continued to ask if we could see the tornado at every Mass we attended with him for years! As John got into middle school, it became less and less often that he would ask if we could see the tornado, to the point where he would go weeks without asking. The last time I remember him asking me if I saw the tornado, he was in seventh grade, and he hadn't asked if we could see the tornado for nearly a year. Suddenly, during the Eucharistic Prayer, John nudged me with his elbow and asked, "Dad, do you see the tornado?" I remember saying back to him, "No, but I really want to!" For 20 years, every time I went to Mass, I knelt there during the Eucharistic prayer watching for that tornado!

After John had first mentioned seeing the tornado at Mass, it made me very curious. I decided to go online, and I did a search for "Angels at Mass," just to see what I could find. I was amazed at what I found! Many saints had witnessed to having similar experiences of seeing angels surround the altar during Mass.

The following are some examples of what I had found…

St. John Chrysostom had said, "When Mass is being celebrated, the Sanctuary is filled with countless Angels who adore the Divine Victim immolated on the altar."

We can read in the revelations of St. Bridget, "One

day when I was assisting at the Holy Sacrifice, I saw an immense number of Holy Angels descend and gather around the altar, contemplating the priest. They sang heavenly canticles that ravished my heart, Heaven itself seemed to be contemplating the great Sacrifice. And yet we poor mortals, blind and miserable creatures, assist at Mass with so little love, relish, and respect!" Do Catholics ever think of this amazing truth, namely: that at Mass they are praying in the midst of thousands of God's Angels?

St. Gertrude had spoken about a day when she decided to offer her reception of Holy Communion in honor of the nine choirs of Angels, and God permitted her to see how radiantly happy and grateful they were for this act of love. She had never dreamed that she could give them such happiness.

St. Augustine is quoted as having said, "The angels surround and help the priest when he is celebrating Mass."

St. Gregory the Great is quoted as having stated the following, "The heavens open and multitudes of angels come to assist in the Holy Sacrifice of the Mass."

Benoîte Rencurel, a shepherdess from Laus, France, saw angels flying in the air above the tabernacle and around the altar during Mass. In her description of this occurrence, she said, "They were laughing as if they were perfectly happy to see the faithful gathered together in prayer."

During his lifetime, St. Padre Pio was known to physically see and have conversations with angels. When asked by some priests, "Are we the only ones who stand around the altar during Mass? Padre Pio responded that God's angels, "the whole celestial court," were found around the altar at Mass.

Henry Suso, the holy Dominican whose cause for canonization is currently taking place, had said, "While I was saying Mass, Angels in visible form gathered around the altar, and some came near to me in raptures of love."

Do we as Catholics ever think about what is actually taking place on the altar during Mass? At Mass, we are sitting, standing, kneeling, and praying while surrounded by a church full of angels!

I also went online to find out what the purpose of an angel is and found the following, as quoted from The Catechism of the Catholic Church…

"The existence of the spiritual, non-corporeal beings that Sacred Scripture usually calls "angels" is a truth of faith.

- 335 In her liturgy, the Church joins with the angels to adore the thrice-holy God.

- 350 Angels are spiritual creatures who glorify God without ceasing.

- 351 The Angels surround Christ their Lord. They serve Him especially in the accomplishment of His saving mission to men."

If Jesus is truly present in the Eucharist, as we as Catholics believe He is, then to me it only makes sense that the church would be filled with angels praising, worshipping, and adoring Him, since that is their job.

"I solemnly assure you, you shall see the sky opened and the angels of God ascending and descending on the Son of Man."
(John 1:51)

Reflection questions:

Have you ever really considered the fact that we are joining the angels and saints in heaven glorifying and praising Christ during the celebration of Mass?

How differently might you look at the Mass knowing that the altar is surrounded by angels, praising and adoring Christ, fully present in the Blessed Sacrament?

Prayer:

Jesus, my Lord, and my God, I believe that your Holy Angels are present at every Mass that is celebrated. May I rejoice and offer praise and adoration with all the angels and saints, knowing that I am in your Holy presence in the Eucharist, at every Mass I attend.

Amen.

The Lamb's Supper

Chapter 6

The Lamb's Supper

During the fall of 2006 and winter/spring of 2007, Betsy and I participated in the aspirancy year of diaconate formation. On Saturday morning, July 7, 2007, we had an interview with then bishop of Green Bay, Bishop David Zubik. This interview would be the final step in the process of getting accepted as a candidate for diaconate formation. Although Bishop Zubik arrived a little late for our interview, seemed a bit distracted, and told us he had had a very difficult week, overall, the interview went well. At the conclusion of the interview, Bishop Zubik told us he would recommend me for candidacy.

Two days later, on Monday morning, July 9, 2007, a press conference was called by the Diocese of Green Bay, and it was announced that Bishop Zubik was to become the twelfth bishop of the Diocese of Pittsburgh. We now understood the distractedness and why Bishop Zubik had a difficult week.

About two weeks later, we received a letter from the Diocese of Green Bay confirming my acceptance as a diaconate formation candidate. In September of 2007, I officially began formation classes as a diaconate candidate.

In the midst of all of this, my friend Mike Reel again invited me to a retreat. This time, however, he invited me to attend a Cursillo, but he didn't have to ask me for five years to get me to say, "Yes." I said, "Yes," right away! On the weekend of September 27-30, 2007, I lived my Cursillo at St. John's Catholic Parish in Menasha, WI.

I thoroughly enjoyed my Cursillo and it was a powerful faith renewal experience, but something permeated the weekend that at the time I didn't understand. The men on the Cursillo spent a great deal of time throughout the weekend excitedly talking about some guy who was coming to speak that week at the local Catholic high school, Appleton Xavier High School. It seemed to be the main topic of discussion whenever we had a break throughout the entire weekend, but for me it meant nothing, because I had never heard of the guy before. It was someone by the name of Scott Hahn. On the evening that Scott Hahn was speaking at Appleton Xavier High School, guess where I ended up going? Not to Appleton Xavier High School. I went to Mishicot to visit my mom.

As my mom and I were talking that evening, she began telling me about an adult faith formation class she had taken over the summer at St. Peter the Fisherman Parish in Two Rivers, WI. The teacher for the class was Sister Jacqueline Spaniola, a friend of ours that we had both gotten to know through Christian Experience Weekend retreats. As my mom was talking about the class, she just kept getting more and more excited about it! She then told me that since I was studying to become a deacon, she thought I needed to read the book they used for the class. My mom walked into her bedroom and came out with a book, which she handed to me. I looked at the cover, and the book was titled, The Lamb's Supper – The Mass as Heaven on Earth. Then I looked at the name of the author…Scott Hahn! A coincidence?

I took the book home and began reading it right away. All I can say is that book changed my life! The amazing thing is it only took five pages into the book for that change to begin. On page 3 it says, "Pope John Paul II has called the Mass 'heaven on earth,' explaining that 'the liturgy we celebrate on earth is a mysterious participation in the heavenly liturgy.'" Dr. Hahn goes on to say, on page 5, "We go to heaven when we go to Mass, and this is true of every single Mass we attend, regardless of the quality of the music, or the fervor of the preaching. The Mass, and I mean, every single Mass, is heaven on earth!" And then he went on to prove it!

He went on to say on page 56 and 57, "In Holy Communion...we receive Him, Whom we praised in the Gloria and proclaimed in the creed! We receive Him, before Whom we swore our solemn oath! We receive Him, Who is the New Covenant awaited through all of human history! When Christ comes at the end of time, He will not have one drop more glory than He has at this moment, when we consume all of Him! In the Eucharist we receive what we will be for all eternity, when we are taken up to heaven to join with the heavenly throng in the marriage supper of the Lamb. At Holy Communion, we are already there. This is not a metaphor. This is the cold, calculated, precise, metaphysical truth that was taught by Jesus Christ."

After reading The Lamb's Supper, I have never looked at the Mass or the Eucharist the same. This is a book that I believe everyone should read, but especially so every single Catholic should read! I believe there would be so much deeper understanding, appreciation, and devotion to the Mass and the Eucharist if all Catholics read it. I believe our church pews would be full for Mass if everyone read this book!

After reading The Lamb's Supper, I began reading more from Scott Hahn, and also anything I could find on the Eucharist. Reading more about Scott Hahn, I found a quote from him that really intrigued me. In it he said, "At Mass, we are not alone, but join with the angels and the saints, as described in the Book of Revelation." My son John having seen angels at Mass continued to make more and more sense to me!

One of the other things I have been drawn to since reading The Lamb's Supper, is the Bread of Life Discourse from the Gospel of John, Chapter 6, which says, "(35) Jesus said to them, "I am the bread of life; whoever comes to me will never hunger, and whoever believes in me will never thirst…(48) I am the bread of life. (49) Your ancestors ate the manna in the desert, but they died; (50) this is the bread that comes down from heaven so that one may eat it and not die. (51) I am the living bread that came down from heaven; whoever eats this bread will live forever; and the bread that I will give is my flesh for the life of the world." (53) Jesus said to them, "Amen, amen, I say to you, unless you eat the flesh of the Son of Man and drink his blood, you do not have life within you. (54) Whoever eats my flesh and drinks my blood has eternal life, and I will raise him on the last day. (55) For my flesh is true food, and my blood is true drink. (56) Whoever eats my flesh and drinks my blood remains in me and I in him. (57) Just as the living Father sent me and I have life because of the Father, so also the one who feeds on me will have life because of me. (58) This is the bread that came down from heaven. Unlike your ancestors who ate and still died, whoever eats this bread will live forever."

The more I read this, the more I realized that this is our faith in a nutshell. This is why we attend Mass and receive the Eucharist.

On a Cursillo, they place each of the men in a table group of six guys you sit with throughout the weekend. This helps to create a small community that you connect with and get to know very well. One of the men at my table was a young man named Kimani who was about 28 years old. Kimani had just been fully received into the Catholic Church the previous Easter Vigil, after having gone through the Rite of Christian Initiation for Adults. Kimani was really on fire, and he challenged all of the men at our table to begin attending daily Mass.

After reading the book from my mom, I was on fire for the Mass and the Eucharist and I found it easy to accept the challenge from Kimani. After speaking to my spiritual director about the desire to attend daily Mass but trying to figure out how to fit it into my work schedule, Father Jim mentioned to me that there was a church, St. Willebrord's Parish, that is three blocks south of the office where I work, and they have a 12:05 p.m. daily Mass which would fit easily into my lunch break. From that point on, if I am in the office over the noon hour, I walk the three blocks down to St. Willebrord's for daily Mass and to receive Jesus in the Eucharist.

> *Then I saw standing in the midst of the throne and the four living creatures and the elders a Lamb that seemed to have been slain. Then I heard every creature in heaven and on earth and under the earth and in the sea, everything in the universe, cry out: "To the one who sits on the throne and to the Lamb be blessing and honor, glory and might, forever and ever."*
> *(Revelation 22:6, 13)*

Reflection question:

At Mass, we participate in the Heavenly Banquet…the Wedding Feast of the Lamb along with every creature in the universe, giving honor, glory, and praise to the Lord… actually experiencing heaven on earth. How will this truth of our Catholic faith impact your participation in the Mass going forward?

Do you attend Mass and receive Jesus in the Blessed Sacrament every Sunday? If not, why?

Do you attend Mass daily? If not, why?

Prayer:

Jesus, Lamb of God,

Open my heart and mind to experience you, fully present in the Eucharist at every Mass. Allow me to fully experience heaven right here on earth at every celebration of the Eucharistic Liturgy in which I participate. I ask this in your Most Holy Name.

Amen.

Bill

CHAPTER 7

Bill

As I began diaconate formation, I was required to meet, one on one, with Deacon Paul Grimm, the diaconate formation director for the Green Bay Diocese, at the conclusion of each academic semester. The men in formation were required to fill out a rather lengthy form called, "Model Standards for Ordination & Post Ordination," prior to our individual meetings with Deacon Paul. The form listed certain standards that the diaconate candidates needed to achieve prior to being ordained. The standards focused on our human, spiritual, intellectual, pastoral, and diaconal growth. By our providing information on our progress regarding each of the standards, the diaconate formation director was able to track how we were doing in our progress toward achieving those standards and we would discuss our progress, or lack of progress, in our meetings together.

In December of 2006, at the end of my first academic semester, I met with Deacon Paul to go over the Model Standards for the very first time. Our conversation centered around the three-fold ministry of a deacon, which includes ministry of the Word, Liturgy, and Charity. Deacon Paul pointed out that at that point in my diaconal formation, I wasn't involved in any ministry of charity. He asked me to pray on what charitable ministry, which would be outreach to those in need or on the fringes of society, that God might be calling me toward. He also suggested to me a number of ministries to consider. One of which was jail ministry.

As I began praying about where God may be leading me, I kept having this nagging thought about jail ministry. I really did not feel drawn to this ministry, but I knew three other deacons – Deacon Rich Bahnaman, Deacon Bob Beehner (both from CEW), and Deacon Cal Naidl, the deacon assigned to our linked parishes – that were all involved in jail ministry together at the Manitowoc County Jail. I also knew a couple other men from CEW, Paul Johnsrud and Steve Sanders, who were also involved.

I spoke to these men about jail ministry, mostly because I thought it might be an easy ministry to get involved in, since it was already established and the men involved in the ministry were all guys I knew. After speaking to each of the men over the next couple of months, I decided that I would give jail ministry a try. The guys gave me information on what I needed to do in order to be able to join the jail ministry team. This included going down to the county jail, providing personal identification, filling out some paperwork, and having a background check done prior to being able to join them. In the spring of 2007, I went to the Manitowoc County Jail to provide all the background information they required. Then I just needed to wait until I passed the background check. Once passed, I was informed I could begin joining the jail ministry team for their weekly Monday evening jail ministry sessions at the facility.

On May 7, 2007, I participated in jail ministry at the Manitowoc County Jail for the very first time. It was a bit unnerving entering the jail that evening. I entered the main entrance of the jail, along with Paul Johnsrud and Steve Sanders. We had to stop at a pass thru window, where the jailers checked our credentials. After verifying we were part of the jail ministry team, we were told we could enter. A large power-operated door opened ahead of us. We all entered through it together. The door slammed shut behind us, leaving us locked in a six-foot-by-six-foot room. A few seconds later, another power-operated door opened on the opposite wall, allowing us to enter into the interior of the jail. As we walked through the doorway into the interior of the jail, the second door slammed shut behind us. At this point, I was not at all feeling comfortable about what I had gotten myself into.

We were now standing in a corridor with a counter on the lefthand side with a large control center beyond it where a number of jailers were watching monitors. On the righthand side of the corridor there was an elevator door. One of the jailers behind the counter pressed a button to call the elevator to our floor. The elevator doors opened and we entered the elevator. When the door closed, the elevator took us up to the third floor. When we got off the elevator, we entered into another corridor. On each end of the corridor there were two doors, each entering into a cell block. There were a series of windows so you could see into the cell blocks and see the incarcerated men inside. On one side of the corridor there was an enclosed control room with jailers in it. On the other side of the corridor was a series of windows that looked into a large room with benches, some tables, a ping-pong table, and some shelves with books. We walked down the corridor to a doorway into the large room. We waited until one of the jailers pressed a button. We could hear a buzzer, indicating that the lock on the door was disengaged. We entered the room, and the door closed and locked behind us. Now my heart was pounding!

Once we were inside the room, we moved the ping pong table and the other tables to the side. We positioned the benches so that they formed a circle in the middle of the room. We put some bibles and other spiritual literature out on the tables, and then waited.

A few minutes later, men in orange jump suits began walking down the corridor from the four cell blocks. They stood outside the door to the room we were in, waiting for the jailer to unlock the door. Another minute or two, and we again hear the buzz at the door, and about 25 to 30 men in orange jump suits entered, greeted us and took a seat on the benches.

Once everyone was seated, Paul and Steve got things started by asking everyone to introduce themselves. Nearly all of the men told us their name, where they were from, gave us a little background on them, as well as telling us why they were in jail. About half of the men local men who were in jail for a short period of time, mostly on drug and alcohol related charges. The other half of the men were from outside of the county, were already sentenced, and were being incarcerated for much more serious crimes. They were being held in the Manitowoc County Jail until a vacancy opened for them in the Wisconsin State Penitentiary System.

I took notice of one of the men right away. He seemed exceptionally quiet, and when it was his turn to introduce himself, he simply said, "I'm Bill, and I'm from Port

Washington." He didn't say another word. As a matter of fact, he didn't say another word the entire evening while we were there.

Our jail ministry session was essentially a scripture study group. We read the readings from Sunday Mass (the previous day's readings). We discussed each of the readings and talked about how the scripture passages related to our individual lives. I was amazed at the depth of faith and the depth of scriptural knowledge many of the men in orange jump suits had. I did not expect to experience that kind of faith in a jail! It was amazing!

At the conclusion of our session, everyone stood up in a circle, held hands, and prayed the Lord's Prayer together. Some of the men grabbed a bible, a missalette, or some other spiritual reading material off of the tables to take with them back to their cells. They then gathered at the door, waiting for the buzzer, so they could head back to their jail cells.

After all the men had left the room, I told Paul and Steve how amazed I was with what I had just experienced. It was not anywhere near as intimidating as I had anticipated it to be. I told them I was definitely coming back the following week. Jail Ministry became a weekly ministry that I thoroughly looked forward to!

As the weeks went by, I couldn't help but notice that when we did introductions each week at the beginning of our jail ministry sessions, the one guy continued to quietly introduce himself as Bill from Port Washington and then proceed to sit silently the rest of the session, never saying another word. This continued for about three months without any change. Then one Monday evening, as we were doing our introductions, we came around to Bill, and he surprised all of us. His introduction that evening began the same way as always, by him saying, "My name is Bill, and I'm from Port Washington." But then, Bill added, "I'm here because I killed someone while driving drunk." He went on to explain that he had grown up in a family with no faith background at all. They didn't own a bible, they never prayed, never talked about God, and certainly never went to church. He said that when he arrived at the Manitowoc County Jail, he was so depressed, because he didn't know how to deal with the guilt he was feeling from having caused someone else's death. He didn't know where to turn or what to do. Then one of the men in his cell block invited him to come to Monday evening jail ministry, because it might help him. He then mentioned that during the previous few months, while attending jail ministry, he began praying, began reading the bible, and it had changed his outlook and his life.

From that point on, Bill began to fully participate in our scripture study on Monday nights. He would volunteer to read the scripture passages and he openly shared his thoughts about how the passages related to what he was going through and how they impacted his life. It was an amazing transformation! What was really cool was how the other men all supported him and his newfound faith!

On Monday evening, December 10, 2007, two weeks before Christmas Eve, as the men were leaving the room following our jail ministry session, Bill came up to Steve Sanders and me and asked if he could speak to us privately. He told us that the following Monday evening would be his last time joining us for our jail ministry sessions. On the following Thursday, he was being transferred to a state penitentiary to complete his sentence. Bill then talked to us about how much his time spent with our group had meant to him. How it had provided him with the gift of faith, which he had never had before. He also told us that he was scared about losing his faith, or falling away from his faith once he left the Manitowoc County Jail. He explained how he had such an amazing support system, between the men in his cell block and all of us that gathered together on Monday evenings, and he didn't know if he would have that at the prison he was being sent to.

Bill then asked us if it would be possible for him to be

baptized before he was transferred? Steve and I looked at each other with huge smiles and said we would talk to Father Dan Felton (now Bishop Felton), a local priest who came into the jail on occasion and provided Mass and Reconciliation for the men. We said we would also discuss it with Deacon Bob Beehner, who was one of the regular members of our jail ministry team, but happened to not be there that evening. Steve and I reached out to Father Dan and Deacon Bob the next day and asked about Bill being able to be baptized.

On Monday evening, December 17, 2007, Steve Sanders, Deacon Bob Beehner, and I arrived together for our weekly jail ministry session. The evening session went well, but was somewhat uneventful, that is, until the conclusion. As always, after completing our usual scripture study, all of the men stood, we held hands, and prayed the Lord's Prayer together. When we finished our prayer, and with all of the men still standing, Deacon Bob walked into the middle of the circle, and asked Bill to join him there. He then asked Bill if it was his desire to be baptized, to which Bill responded, it was.

At this point, Deacon Bob began praying the prayers of the Rite of Baptism. Deacon Bob had brought a capped, liter bottle of Holy Water with him, and proceeded to baptize Bill, right there in the middle of that third-floor room in the Manitowoc County Jail! Deacon Bob prayed the Sacramental words of baptism, saying, "Bill, I baptize you, in the name of the Father, and of the Son, and of the Holy Spirit," pouring the entire contents of the liter bottle of Holy Water over Bill's head, right there in the middle of the circle of men!

As I watched Bill being baptized, the biggest smile I think I have ever seen covered Bill's face. He was glowing. It was as if you could see the presence of the Holy Spirit fill him up! I then looked around the circle, at the group of about 30 grown men wearing orange jump suits, and there was not a single one of them that did not have tears running down their cheeks.

But the thing that was just as amazing happened as the men began to leave the room to head back to their cell blocks. One by one, the men wearing orange jump suits walked to the middle of the room, got down on their knees, placed their hand in the Holy Water that had spilled all over the floor during Bill's baptism, and signed themselves with the sign of the cross. At this point, Steve, Deacon Bob, and I were all in tears.

We hugged and congratulated Bill before he headed back to his cell, and he could not stop smiling! He thanked us over and over for providing him the opportunity to be baptized, but also for allowing it to occur with all of the men present who had such a big part in his conversion to the faith.

That was the last time I saw Bill, but I think of him and pray for him very often. As big of an influence as jail ministry was in Bill's conversion and baptism, he has no idea the impact he had on me during those seven months in 2007, when we both walked that journey of faith, and grew in our faith together.

> *Go, therefore, and make disciples of all nations, baptizing them in the name of the Father, and of the Son, and of the holy Spirit, teaching them to observe all that I have commanded you. And behold, I am with you always, until the end of the age." (Matthew 28:19-20)*

Reflection questions:

Are you living your day-to-day life in a Christian manner that signifies that you believe Jesus is with you always, even to the end of time?

As a baptized Christian, are you living out your baptismal calling to make disciples of all people?

In what ways are you helping to teach others to observe all that Jesus has commanded you?

In what ways are you helping lead others to a conversion of heart?

Have you had a profound experience either during your own baptism, or in witnessing someone else's baptism?

Prayer:

Lord Jesus, I pray that through the power of the Holy Spirit, I can grow in confidence to lead others to a conversion of heart, a metanoia. Help me to boldly witness to your presence in my life, to teach others to observe all You have commanded me, to live my life as an example of your true and holy presence living in me and in our world.

Amen.

Forming a New Community

CHAPTER 8

Forming a New Community

During the summer of 2008 I received an email from Deacon Bob Beehner, the spiritual director for the Manitowoc Christian Experience Weekend retreat community, known at this point as Lakeshore CEW. Deacon Bob said one of the original goals of the Lakeshore CEW community was to eventually expand Christian Experience Weekend retreats to other communities. Because the community had grown fairly large, and there were community members from other cities and areas around Northeast Wisconsin, they felt it might be a good time to explore their goal of expansion. Deacon Bob invited CEW community members to a meeting during the first week of August to brainstorm ideas for communities to potentially expand to.

I attended the meeting, and suggested they expand to the Denmark area, since All Saints Parish had facilities that would easily work for holding a weekend retreat, plus it is only a 30-minute drive from Manitowoc, making it easy for the Manitowoc community to be available to help plan and put on the retreat weekends. With Denmark being only 15 miles from Green Bay, it would also give us a larger population to draw retreat candidates from.

God had actually placed this desire on my heart years earlier while on my second CEW retreat. I had given a great deal of thought about how the facilities at All Saints would work very well for holding a CEW at our parish. This was a perfect opportunity to make that desire a reality!

My suggestion was also somewhat selfish. I felt that by having Christian Experience Weekend retreats in Denmark – only five minutes from home – it would make it much easier for me to get more involved and really immerse myself in both the men's and women's retreat weekends. I also figured it would make it much easier to convince my friends and fellow parishioners in the Denmark area to attend a weekend retreat.

It was agreed upon at the meeting to begin looking into holding Christian Experience Weekend retreats in Denmark. The first step in the process would be getting approval to start a CEW community in our linked parishes, as well as approval from All Saints Parish to hold retreats in their parish facilities.

I reached out to the Circle of Faith Catholic Community Joint Pastoral Councils, asking to be put on their joint council meeting agenda. The Circle of Faith Catholic community was at that time, a group of four linked parishes in the Denmark area, all served by the same pastor, Father Ron Colombo. The Circle of Faith Catholic Community included All Saints Parish in Denmark, St. James Parish in Cooperstown, St. Joseph Parish in Kellnersville, and Holy Trinity Parish in New Denmark.

In September of 2008, me and six other members of Lakeshore CEW community met with the Circle of Faith Catholic Community Joint Pastoral Councils. After witnessing to the Joint Pastoral Councils to what Christian Experience Weekend retreats were, and witnessing to the positive results that Christian Experience Weekends had had in Manitowoc, we requested permission to begin holding Christian Experience Weekend Retreats at All Saints Parish in Denmark. The Joint Pastoral Councils gave their unanimous approval to begin initial expansion planning. As a matter of fact, one of the Council members was so impressed by our witnessing that he offered to make a personal financial donation to be used as seed money to help get Christian Experience Weekends started in the Circle of Faith!

I was asked to witness to the effect of Christian

Experience Weekends on my life and the lives of so many others at each of the Circle of Faith Catholic Community weekend Masses on the last weekend of September of 2008. My witnessing at Masses resulted in a total of five men and 13 women from the Circle of Faith Catholic Community attending Lakeshore CEWs during the fall of 2008 and winter of 2009.

During May of 2009, we began meeting with those who had attended a CEW from The Circle of Faith, and a large group of men and women from the Lakeshore CEW community. We started the planning for upcoming Denmark Area Christian Experience Weekend retreats and to choose a leadership team to lead the retreats. I was asked to lead the group as our first men's rector and accepted, though I also felt obligated since I had been the one who had requested expanding CEW to the Denmark area. Cathie Lodel, a CEW veteran from St. Joseph's Parish in Kellnersville, volunteered to be the rector for our women's retreat. We had one couple, Dan and Suzanne Zellner, members of All Saints Parish, as well as Cathy Duescher from St. James Parish volunteer to be assistant rectors, meaning they would also be future rectors. All three of them had only attended one CEW, prior to volunteering. As a group, we agreed to reach out to Paul Johnsrud, a CEW veteran from Lakeshore CEW, and invite him to join our group as an assistant rector. Paul happily agreed!

The first Denmark Area CEW, a men's retreat weekend, was held on the weekend of September 25-27, 2009, and the first women's retreat weekend was held on the weekend of February 19-21, 2010. Both retreats had teams made up of members of the Lakeshore CEW community, Circle of Faith Catholic Community men and women who had previously experienced a Christian Experience Weekend, and men and women who had attended a Cursillo retreat from the Circle of Faith Catholic Community.

Thanks be to God, and to the hard work of so many people from both the Lakeshore CEW community and the Circle of Faith Catholic Community, our first Denmark Area CEW Weekends were huge successes! I experienced a beautiful example of faith-filled people joining together as a community to love and serve the Lord for the benefit of others. Our first retreat weekends were filled with the presence of the Holy Spirit and if I had not known better, they would have seemed more like our 20th weekends in Denmark rather than our first and second.

Although I was excited to begin holding, and then to have held the retreats at our parish in Denmark, little did I know just how huge of an effect the Denmark Area Christian Experience Weekend retreats, and the Denmark

Christian Experience Weekend retreat community would have on my ongoing faith journey and how much it would be integral in the amazing spiritual experiences I was yet to encounter!

> *Every day they devoted themselves to meeting together in the temple area and to breaking bread in their homes. They ate their meals with exultation and sincerity of heart, praising God and enjoying favor with all the people. And every day the Lord added to their number those who were being saved.*
> *(Acts 2:46-47)*

Reflection questions:

From the beginning, Christianity has been centered around gathering as community. How has your life been influenced by a Christian community?

What type of small Christian communities have, or are you a part of…Bible study group, prayer group, ministry group, etc.? If you aren't part of a Christian Community, where may God be calling you to become involved in one?

Prayer:

Lord Jesus, beloved of my soul, Open my eyes and heart to see how you are actively walking this faith journey with me. May my heart be open to go where you are calling me, and how you may be calling me to form or participate in a small Christian community that shares their faith with one another. Place the desire in my heart to do the things you are calling me to do. I promise to submit myself to your will and where you are leading me.

Amen.

Ordination

CHAPTER 9

Ordination

In the weeks leading up to my ordination, I experienced what I can only describe as a spiritual attack. I had nearly constant thoughts of not being good enough to actually be ordained a deacon in the Catholic Church. I had doubts, even after having completed six years of formation, whether God was actually calling me to be ordained a deacon. These doubts and questions made it difficult to focus on work and also kept me awake at night. I realize, looking back, that Satan was working hard on me, trying to prevent me from going through with ordination. It wasn't until the day before my ordination, after weeks of prayer, when during noon Mass at St. Willebrord's Parish I finally had the feeling come over me that God was absolutely calling me to ordination, that I was in the right place, doing the right thing. There was a complete sense of peace that came over me during that Mass.

It was at a 10 a.m. Mass on Saturday, May 19, 2012, at St. Francis Xavier Cathedral in Green Bay, that I was ordained a deacon by Bishop David L. Ricken. I was assigned by Bishop Ricken to serve as deacon at The Circle of Faith

Catholic Community, which had by this time expanded to include the parishes of All Saints in Denmark, St. James in Cooperstown, St. Joseph's in Kellnersville, Holy Trinity in New Denmark, and St. Mary's Parish with worship sites in Glenmore and Stark. That's five parishes with six worship sites, all served by one priest, Father Ron Colombo!

Throughout the entire ordination Mass, also known as the Rite of Ordination to the Order of Deacon, I was extremely emotional. The emotions began with the processional song, Here I Am Lord. This song always gets me emotional and it has ever since my first Christian Experience Weekend retreat. Near the end of that retreat weekend, Here I Am Lord, was played, and the lyrics of the song expressed to me, in a sense, my call to the diaconate. The lyrics, "Here I am Lord, is it I Lord, I have heard you calling in the night," brought me right back to that winter evening in 1993, while driving in my car, when I heard the voice of God telling me that He wanted me to be a deacon. As the lyrics continued, "I will go Lord, if you lead me, I will hold your people in my heart," the words pierced my heart. It was at that moment on that CEW retreat that I knew I had to go talk to Father Ron Colombo about becoming a deacon when I returned home from the retreat.

As the processional song for the ordination Mass began and we started the procession into the cathedral, my emotions took over, and I began to sob. I continued to cry all the way up the aisle. As I got to my pew, where Betsy and my children were already waiting, Betsy grabbed my hand and smiled at me, knowing why I was emotional. Her smile gave me an amazing sense of peace.

Following the homily, the elect – the men who are about to be ordained – each individually kneel before the bishop, place their hands in his, and promise respect and obedience to the bishop and his successors. Immediately following this, the Litany of the Saints is sung. During the Litany of the Saints, the elect lie prostrate on the sanctuary floor directly in front of the altar. As I was lying on the floor, and the entire assembly in the cathedral was invoking the prayers of the saints in song on behalf of us, the elect, I again began sobbing. It was perhaps the most emotional moment of my entire life as I felt this amazing bond to all the saints who have come before us, paving the way for our faith today. It felt like all the saints were right there with us at that moment!

Immediately following the Litany of Saints, there is the part of the rite known as the Laying On of Hands and the Prayer of Consecration. By the Laying On of Hands and the Prayer of Consecration, the grace of the Sacrament of Holy Orders is both requested and conferred by the power of the Holy Spirit acting in the Church. The Laying On of Hands is specifically the invocation of the Holy Spirit. Each of the diaconate candidates kneels before the bishop who lays his hands on their heads in silence.

The Prayer of Consecration follows the Laying On of Hands and recalls the vocation of the first seven men to assist the apostles in their daily ministry so that they could devote themselves more fully to prayer and the preaching of the Word. The prayer is directed to God, who by the power of the Holy Spirit, provides for the various forms of ministry within the Church. It asks that the grace of the seven gifts of the Holy Spirit be sent upon the candidates for the faithful carrying out of the ministry of the deacon. The prayer also asks that every Gospel virtue abound in each deacon so his concern will be for the sick and the poor. Once this prayer is concluded, those being ordained are now deacons.

In the Laying On of Hands during my ordination, as I knelt before Bishop Ricken and he placed his hands on my head, something amazing happened! As Bishop Ricken placed his hands on my head for approximately eight seconds, I could feel what felt like some sort of power and warmth enter into my body from his fingertips. It began at my head and slowly washed through my body right down to the tips of my toes. An overwhelming sense of peace came over me as this occurred!

There is no doubt in my mind that I physically felt the Holy Spirit entering into my being, and filling me up with His presence, power, and fire! I have never felt anything that could compare to that amazing feeling! This was an even more powerful feeling than I had felt at that first CEW when I experienced the fire of the Holy Spirit for the first time!

After the ordination Mass, I was speaking to one of the men who was ordained with me, and he told me he had the exact same feeling wash over him during the Laying On of Hands. As I have stated before, if you have never had such an encounter, I pray that you too can have the experience of having your heart set on fire by the Holy Spirit!

Prior to my call to the diaconate, I really didn't have what I would consider a strong relationship with Jesus. When I prayed, I typically directed my prayers to God the Father, rarely to Jesus, and never to the Holy Spirit. As I look back now, it has become very evident to me that as I began praying the Rosary, I was developing a very strong devotion to the Blessed Virgin Mary. As a result, it was Mary who was bringing me into relationship with her son, Jesus, which eventually became a very strong, personal relationship with Jesus. That relationship in turn led me to profoundly experience the presence, power, and fire of the Holy Spirit in my life. Thank you, Mary, for leading me to your son, and to your spouse, the Holy Spirit!

> *Then they laid hands on them,*
> *and they received the Holy Spirit.*
> *(Acts 8:17)*

Reflection questions:

The Holy Spirit is invoked as part of every Sacrament of the Church. How have you experienced the presence of the Holy Spirit in the Sacraments?

How have you experienced the presence, power and fire of the Holy Spirit in your life, outside of a Sacramental experience?

When you pray, do you pray to the Holy Spirit? If not, consider making the Prayer to the Holy Spirit part of your daily prayers, asking Him daily to set your heart on fire.

Prayer to the Holy Spirit

Come Holy Spirit, fill the hearts of your faithful and kindle in them the fire of your love. Send forth your Spirit, and they shall be created, and You shall renew the face of the earth.

Let us pray. O, God, who by the light of the Holy Spirit, did instruct the hearts of the faithful, grant that by the same Holy Spirit we may be truly wise and ever enjoy His consolations.

Through Christ Our Lord.

Amen.

Mother Mary Comes to Me

CHAPTER 10

Mother Mary Comes to Me

A GOOD FRIEND OF MINE, JIM GILLIS, HAS BEEN A SPIRItual mentor ever since I first met him. Jim is a man of very deep faith. He attended seminary and was ordained a transitional deacon in the Catholic Church but was never ordained to the priesthood. He has a great deal of theological knowledge and has had some spiritual experiences that blow me away. Jim also has the deepest devotion to the Blessed Virgin Mary of anyone I know. He is a very intense man when it comes to his faith life and discipleship, and as a result, he sometimes spiritually intimidates people.

For me, it is just the opposite. I gravitate toward Jim. I believe God has placed him in my life to strengthen my faith and keep me accountable. Over the years that I have known Jim, he constantly challenges me to go further and dig deeper into my faith, and does not allow me to grow stagnant in my faith. If Jim doesn't agree with me about something faith related, he will tell me so, and challenges me to look at things from a slightly different perspective. I have found that because I am a deacon, most people won't challenge me, or question me, but Jim will, and thank God that he does, as he has helped me grow deeply in my spiritual life.

Jim also is one of only a few people I know who is blessed with a number of spiritual gifts, including the ability to pray in tongues. Praying in tongues is a charismatic gift of the Holy Spirit where the person given this gift prays in a language they don't know or understand. Jim has told me that he was once told that he is speaking in Yiddish when he prays in tongues. Yiddish is a German dialect which integrates many languages and is used by Jewish people in Central and Eastern Europe. Jim has prayed over me in tongues on a number of occasions, and when he has done so, it is one of the most amazing, peaceful feelings I have ever experienced.

Because of Jim's deep devotion to the Blessed Virgin Mary, during the summer of 2013, a group of people from our Christian Experience Weekend community, led by the encouragement of Jim Gillis and his wife Gail, and husband and wife Sam and Nicole Hall, suggested that we offer something new to our retreat community as well as to the parishioners of our linked parishes. It was a do-it-yourself retreat experience titled "33 Days to Morning Glory," presented by Father Michael E. Gaitley, MIC. The retreat is a 33-day preparation to consecrating yourself to Jesus through the Virgin Mary. We had 18 people, mostly couples, sign up and participate in the retreat, including Betsy and me.

The retreat includes daily reading and journaling, gathering together once a week as a group to watch a 20- to 30-minute video that recaps the previous week's studies, and prepares you for the coming week's daily reading assignments. The weekly gathering also includes group discussion about that week's topic. At the conclusion of the retreat, the entire group consecrates themselves individually to Jesus through Mary.

The retreat book that we used includes a "cheat sheet" for starting dates for the retreat and dates for consecration so the consecration date lands on a Marian Feast Day. We began our retreat on Saturday July 13, 2013, so that our consecration day would take place on Thursday, Aug. 15, 2013, which is the Solemnity of the Assumption of Mary.

During the retreat we studied the lives and teachings of four amazing saints who had a deep devotion to Mary. They included St. Louis de Montfort, St. Maximilian Kolbe, St. Mother Teresa of Calcutta, and St. John Paul II. Learning about, and through these amazing saints, drew me into a deeper devotion to Mary.

On our consecration day, our group attended morning Mass together at All Saints Church. Father Ron Colombo gave us all a blessing, and after communion we all prayed our prayer of consecration and each participant in the retreat placed a rose at the feet of the statue of Mary in church. It was a deeply spiritually emotional experience for me and sharing that experience with Betsy was amazing!

Since going through the "33 Days to Morning Glory" retreat, there is no doubt in my mind that Mary has and continues to lead me into a deeper relationship with her son Jesus. It has also become evident that in growing deeper in my relationship with Jesus that the Holy Spirit has continued to open my heart and mind to the truth of Jesus' full and complete presence in the Blessed Sacrament. Over the next number of years, that opening of my heart and mind was only going to increase.

> *When Elizabeth heard Mary's greeting, the infant leaped in her womb, and Elizabeth, filled with the Holy Spirit, cried out in a loud voice, and said, "Most blessed are you among women, and blessed is the fruit of your womb. And how does this happen to me, that the mother of my Lord should come to me?"*
> *(Luke 1:41-43)*

Reflection questions:

How is your relationship with Mary, the Mother of God?

Do you regularly participate in any Marian devotions?

How are you allowing Mary to draw you into a deeper relationship with her son Jesus?

It is Mary's God-given mission to help us become saints. Are you allowing Mary and asking her to intercede on your behalf to help you live a more saintly life?

Prayer: *Since my consecration day, I begin my morning prayers each day by renewing my consecration to Jesus through Mary by praying the following prayer, found in the "33 Days to Morning Glory" book:*

Mary, I want to be a saint. I know that you also want me to be a saint and that it's your God-given mission to form me into one. So, Mary, at this moment, on this day I freely choose to give you my full permission to do your work in me, with your Spouse, the Holy Spirit.

Amen.

Blessed By Jesus

CHAPTER 11

Blessed By Jesus

While in Diaconate formation, one of the ministries I began to get involved in and was very passionate about was youth ministry. After ordination, I took over as youth minister in our linked parishes. We no longer had a three-person youth minister team. During my time as youth minister, we continually tried to expand the youth ministry program, which meant also including middle school students into our program.

The Archdiocese of Milwaukee has an annual Catholic youth rally called St. John Bosco Youth Day. It is held at Holy Hill Basilica and National Shrine to Mary Help of Christians, in Hubertus, WI, located in the Archdiocese of Milwaukee about 30 miles northwest of Milwaukee.

In the fall of 2013, the Diocese of Green Bay Youth Ministry Department invited youth ministers and their youth ministry program participants from around the diocese to attend St. John Bosco Youth Day. The diocese provided a fleet of buses to transport middle and high school students and youth ministers from around the diocese down to Holy Hill. On Saturday, October 5, 2013, my wife Betsy and I, along with another couple, Patrick and Jessica Phillips, were chaperones for about 20 middle and high school students from our youth ministry program who attended St. John Bosco Youth Day.

When we arrived, we found that there were approximately 2,000 middle and high school students from the five dioceses around the state of Wisconsin at this event. They had a tent set up with about 25 Reconciliation stations in it for anyone who wanted to take advantage of the Sacrament of Reconciliation. There was another tent set up as a Eucharistic Adoration Chapel. There was a very large tent set up with seating for about 2,000, and had a large stage set up on one side of the tent. This large tent probably could have covered two football fields.

The keynote speakers and musicians for the event were Catholic heavy hitters, although at the time, I hadn't heard of any of them. Joel Stepanek, the Life Support Coordinator at Life Teen was the emcee for the day.

Two of the speakers were Jackie Francois Angel, an internationally known Catholic speaker, singer, and songwriter, and her husband Bobby Angel, a campus minister and theology teacher.

Musician Ike Ndolo, an internationally known Catholic

singer and songwriter, along with his band, provided praise and worship music, as well as music for Mass that day, with some help on vocals from Jackie Francois Angel.

Archbishop Jerome Listecki, from the Archdiocese of Milwaukee, was the main celebrant and homilist for Mass.

Father Mike Schmitz, the Director of Youth and Young Adult Ministry for the Diocese of Duluth Minnesota and the Newman Center Chaplain at the University of Minnesota Duluth, and now well known for his Ascension Presents videos online, was the keynote speaker.

During the middle of the afternoon, Father Mike Schmitz processed the Blessed Sacrament within the monstrance from the Adoration Tent into the main tent for Eucharistic Adoration, with Ike Ndolo providing music. As part of the Eucharistic procession, Father Mike was led by a cross bearer, and there were four candle bearers – two in front of Father Mike and two behind him. There were also four priests carrying a canopy that covered the blessed Sacrament. Father Mike placed the monstrance on an altar on the stage, and we had about 20 minutes of Eucharistic Adoration in the main tent, with soft background music being played by Ike Ndolo.

After about 20 minutes, Father Mike again began a Eucharistic procession, but this time around the inside of the tent. He again had the cross bearer leading the procession, and four candle bearers processing with him. As Father Mike was processing around the tent, Ike Ndolo was playing Matt Maher's song "Adoration", which is the Tantum Ergo. At the time I hadn't yet heard Matt Maher's recording of "Adoration," although I would become very familiar with it over the next few years.

Father Mike processed the Blessed Sacrament in the monstrance up and down the aisles between the seating in the tent, stopping in the aisle about every 15 rows of chairs, and blessing the people with the Blessed Sacrament.

I was sitting on the end of the row along the aisle. As Father Mike processed up our aisle, he stopped about two rows in front of me to do the blessing. As he stopped, I heard an audible gasp from across the aisle to my left. I turned and looked, and there were two young men sitting directly across the aisle from me. I don't know who they were, but they looked to be about 15 or 16 years old. Both young men fell to their knees and began sobbing. As Father Mike blessed us with the Blessed Sacrament, the two young men fell flat on their faces on the ground and laid there and sobbed. It was a rainy day, and the grass inside the tent was damp and kind of muddy, but it didn't matter to these two young men. They just laid there in the mud crying.

As the Eucharistic procession went past us, I remember looking at those two young men laying there crying and thinking to myself –well, actually praying, "Lord, I want what these two young men have! I want to be that passionate about Jesus Christ in the Eucharist that I become emotional and am moved to tears in the presence of the Blessed Sacrament!"

When I prayed those words on the rainy, October Saturday afternoon, little did I know that God would answer that prayer profoundly in my life. And not only that, but he would answer it over, and over again!

Not too long after my ordination, a group of people, including me, started a ministry group called Exploration Ministries. Exploration Ministries' mission was to offer day retreat experiences that explored the Catholic Faith and would aid individuals in education and their personal relationship with God. The very first day retreat that we offered took place at All Saints Parish in Denmark on Saturday, October 26, 2013, just three weeks after having attended the St. John Bosco Youth Day. The theme of the retreat was "The Eucharist - The Source and Summit of our Faith." I was asked by our group to be a keynote speaker for the retreat. I was on fire for the Eucharist after attending St. John Bosco Youth Day. As part of my talk, I shared the story of my son John having seen angels at Mass and was overwhelmed by the emotional reaction people had!

As a result of that talk, over the next few years, I began to be asked by religious education coordinators at surrounding parishes to share the story about my son with students in their confirmation classes. I was just beginning what has been an amazing spiritual journey.

Come, then, let us bow down and worship;
Bending the knee before the LORD our maker.
For he is our God, we are His people, the flock he shepherds.
(Psalm 95:6-7)

Reflection questions:

How do you respond/react when in the presence of Christ in the Blessed Sacrament, whether at Mass, at Eucharistic Adoration, or in his presence in the tabernacle?

St. John Paul II wrote in his 1980 Apostolic Letter, Dominicae Cenae, "The Church and the world have a great need for Eucharistic worship. Jesus waits for us in the Sacrament of love…Let us be generous with our time in going to meet Him in Adoration…" Is Eucharistic Adoration a regular part of the practice of your faith, and if not, have you ever considered making it a regular practice?

Prayer for Eucharistic Adoration:

> I adore You, Bread from Heaven.
> I adore You, Bread of Angels.
> I adore You, Jesus, truly present in the Blessed Sacrament.
> I adore You, Jesus, my true life because you died for me.
> I adore You, Jesus, Divine Light,
> because You show me the way to heaven.
> I adore You, Jesus, The Lamb of God,
> who takes away the sin of the world.
> My God and Savior, Jesus Christ, true God and true Man.
> I believe that you are really and bodily present
> in the Blessed Sacrament on the altar.
> From the very depths of my heart, I adore You.
> Amen.

The Blood of Christ

CHAPTER 12

The Blood of Christ

On July 1, 2014, Father Ron Colombo was granted senior priest status by Bishop Ricken, and our linkage was split into two separate linkages. I was assigned to the linked parishes of All Saints in Denmark, Holy Trinity in New Denmark, and St. Mary's, Glenmore and Stark, and we were assigned a new parish priest, Father Kevin Ori.

On the weekend of October 15, 2017, I was serving as deacon at all the masses in our linkage and was preaching the homily that weekend. The Gospel reading that I preached on was about a king, who gave a wedding feast for his son. He asked his servants to invite the guests, but they did not show up.

In my homily I spoke about how we have the opportunity to experience the Wedding Feast of Heaven – heaven on earth – every time we come to Mass. I also spoke about my experience with my mom giving me Scott Hahn's book, The Lamb's Supper – The Mass as Heaven on Earth.

At the consecration, or Eucharistic Prayer during Mass, Father Kevin would have wine poured into the chalice, but would also have a glass decanter with wine in it placed on the Corporal, next to the Chalice. The wine in the glass decanter would then be consecrated into the Blood of Christ at the Eucharistic Prayer. Following the consecration, but before communion, the wine in the glass decanter would be poured into the common cups that would be used for distributing the Blood of Christ to the faithful in the pews as they came up for communion.

This particular weekend, at the 4 p.m. Saturday Mass at All Saints Parish, as Father Kevin began praying the Eucharistic prayer and as I knelt to the right-hand side of Father Kevin at the altar, I noticed a drop of something running down the inside of the long neck of the decanter and into the wine. At first, I thought to myself, "there must have been a drop of wine on the rim of the bottle that ran down," but then I noticed that another drop ran down the neck of the bottle, and then another, and yet another. Pretty soon there were drops running down the inside of the bottle, all the way around the neck of the bottle – just basically appearing from the rim of the bottle. The more I looked at those drops, the more I realized that they didn't look like wine, they looked like blood running down into the wine! It kept running, mixing with the wine. As I knelt there and continued to watch this happen, my eyes filled with tears. As soon as Father Kevin concluded the

Eucharistic prayer, the flowing of the drops of blood instantly stopped! I remember thinking to myself, "Did I really just see that? Was that real?" I had tears in my eyes for the remainder of the Mass as I reflected on what had just happened.

Two hours later, at the next Mass that evening, 6 p.m. Saturday Mass at Holy Trinity Parish, Father Kevin was using a similar, but different, decanter and the very same thing happened during the Eucharistic Prayer. Again, I began to cry as I watched the drops of blood run down the inside of the long neck of the glass decanter. After witnessing the identical thing happening just two hours apart, there was no doubt in my mind that I was seeing the blood of the crucified Jesus running down the inside of those bottles, mixing with the wine, and changing the wine into the real blood of Jesus.

I don't recall if it was that same evening, or the following day, on Sunday afternoon, but my friend, Dan Gray (now Deacon Dan Gray), who also has been very active in our Denmark Area CEW community, called me to tell me what he had experienced at Mass that weekend. Dan was in diaconate formation at the time. Dan shared with me that he had attended Mass at St. James Parish in Cooperstown and that he had had a remarkable experience during the Eucharistic Prayer. He told me that as the priest elevated the Host at the consecration, that he had seen a bright flash of light come from the host. I then shared with Dan what I had witnessed at the two Masses on Saturday evening.

We both found it amazing that we both had such very profound experiences in the presence of the Eucharist at Mass on the same weekend. God is good!

> *Then he took a cup, gave thanks, and gave it to them, saying, "Drink from it, all of you, for this is my blood of the covenant, which will be shed on behalf of many for the forgiveness of sins." (Matthew 26:28)*

Reflection questions:

How has the Blood of Christ cleansed you?

In what way has Christ's shedding of His blood on the cross impacted your participation on the Eucharist?

Deacon David Scheuer

Prayer:

Merciful and Gracious Lord,
Have mercy on me for my sins.
I pray for Your forgiveness for all of my sins,
And beg you to wash them away with
The Precious Blood of Christ.
I thank you for your mercy, compassion, and protection.
I offer this prayer in the name of Jesus, my Lord and Savior.

Amen.

Pulling Back
the Veil

CHAPTER 13

Pulling Back the Veil

JUST OVER FOUR MONTHS AFTER HAVING EXPERIENCED the blood running down the neck of the wine decanters at Mass, another amazing and emotional encounter was about to occur.

On the weekend of February 23-25 of 2018, we were hosting our Women's Christian Experience Weekend retreat at All Saints Parish in Denmark. Through the suggestion and encouragement of Jim Gillis, we set up and make a part of our retreat weekends an Adoration Chapel in the room that once was the chapel in the former Sisters' residence attached to our parish school. We expose the Blessed Sacrament in the monstrance on an altar set up in the chapel for 24-hour around the clock adoration to take place the entire time the retreat is going. We ask members of our Christian Experience Weekend retreat community who are not attending the retreat to fill time slots throughout the weekend so that we always have at least two people praying before the Blessed Sacrament from the time the retreat candidates begin to arrive at 7 p.m. on Friday, until the retreatants celebrate Sunday Mass at 2 p.m. in another chapel that we set up in one of the classrooms of our parish school. The Adoration Chapel has a separate entrance available so the community members coming in to pray in the Adoration Chapel aren't seen by those on the retreat, and the new retreat candidates aren't even aware that this ministry is taking place in the building while they are on retreat.

On Friday at 7 p.m., as the retreat is just beginning, we have a Eucharistic procession with the monstrance and candle bearers as we bring the Blessed Sacrament from the church to the Adoration Chapel. The Eucharistic Procession processes from the church, down a flight of stairs into the church basement. It then crosses the parish hall in the church basement to another half flight of stairs that goes down into a tunnel passage beneath the driveway between the church and school, leading to the parish school basement. The procession then crosses the church basement and goes up a flight of stairs into the first floor of the school. At the top of the stairs, the procession turns to the right, through a doorway, into what used to be the Sisters' residence and is now used as our parish office building. The procession then goes down a short corridor, through another doorway where it then turns to the right and about eight feet ahead is another door on the righthand side that enters into our Adoration Chapel.

At 2 p.m. on Sunday, as the retreatants begin their celebration of Sunday Mass, we have another Eucharistic procession, bringing the Blessed Sacrament in the monstrance back to church following the same route, where we repose the Blessed Sacrament back into the Tabernacle. When the Eucharistic Procession gets to church, and prior to reposing the Blessed Sacrament in the Tabernacle, we always celebrate Benediction of the Blessed Sacrament.

This particular Sunday afternoon, February 25, 2018, as a deacon, I was the one processing the Blessed Sacrament back to church and leading Benediction. I had four candle bearers with me. Two were ahead of me leading the procession and two were directly behind me. There were also five or six other men that processed with us back to church and remained for Benediction. We began Benediction by playing and singing Matt Maher's song "Adoration", which again, is the Tantum Ergo. I was kneeling before the altar as the music began playing.

As I knelt before the Blessed Sacrament, about six feet in front of the altar, I noticed something spinning around the perimeter of the altar in a clockwise motion at a very high rate of speed. I could see through it, because I could still see the monstrance on the altar, but there was something definitely spinning around the altar, and it was physically moving between me and the altar. As I tried to focus in on what it was, the only thing that was obvious is that it was sparkling with very bright light!

Suddenly it stopped. It immediately started spinning the opposite direction around the altar. Suddenly it stopped again, but now I could see what looked like bodily figures surrounding the altar! I immediately realized what I was witnessing! I just witnessed the tornado that my son John had seen, and I was now seeing angels! The angels completely surrounded the altar. As I said, I could see them and could make out what they were, but at the same time I could see through them as I could still see the monstrance on the altar. The angels continued to sparkle with very bright light! As I was watching the angels, they suddenly began swaying back and forth to the rhythm of the music. It was as if they were actually dancing before the Lord, fully present on the altar in the Blessed Sacrament! As I watched all of this taking place right before me, I began sobbing and could not continue to sing. It was not something that was frightening, or uncomfortable. Rather, I had this overwhelming sense of peace come over me, but I was crying uncontrollably.

As soon as the song ended, the angels just simply disappeared. I continued to sob uncontrollably at this point, but I was the one leading Benediction. Even though I was crying heavily, I had to pray the prayers of Benediction, including the divine praises. I just cried my way through them.

When I had completed Benediction and had reposed the Blessed Sacrament in the tabernacle, the men who were there with me for Benediction asked if I was OK. I told them what had happened, that I had just witnessed the tornado and saw angels dancing around the altar, but none of them had seen any of what I had just seen. Needless to say, there were a lot of hugs and tears shared. I said to Dan Valenta, one of the men who was there with me, "I don't even know what to do with this!" He simply smiled, looked me square in the eye, and said to me, "You have to share it".

I then walked out of the church and walked into the parking lot behind the church. I leaned up against my car and stood out there for quite a while and just cried. While I was still crying, Father Mark Mleziva, at the time one of our newly ordained diocesan priests, came walking out of the side door of the school into the parking lot. Father Mark had been in the school in the classroom chapel presiding at Sunday Mass for the women on retreat. As he walked out of the side door of the school, he saw me standing by my car and came walking over to me. Father Mark noticed I was crying and asked what was wrong. I told him that while celebrating Benediction of the Blessed

Sacrament, that I had seen a tornado of angels around the altar, and then watched as they danced before Jesus in the Blessed Sacrament.

Father Mark got a huge smile on his face and said to me, "Do you realize how blessed you are? Every once in a while, God will pull back the veil just a tiny bit and give us a little glimpse of heaven. You just experienced heaven on earth! You are so blessed!" Father Mark gave me a big hug, climbed in his car, and left. I was again standing there crying, all alone, out in the parking lot on that cold February afternoon. Yet I did not feel at all cold, even though I was not wearing a jacket.

The following day, Monday Feb. 26, 2018, I went to noon Mass at St. Willebrord's Parish in downtown Green Bay, as I try to do every day that I am in the office for work. During Mass, I was somewhat preoccupied thinking about what I had witnessed on Sunday afternoon. As Father Andy Cribben, the pastor at St. Willebrord's began praying the Eucharistic Prayer, I was kneeling there, again watching for the tornado, watching for the angels. All of the sudden, I heard a voice – an audible voice – the same voice that I had heard some fifteen years earlier that said, "Dave, I want you to be a deacon!" But this time the voice said to me, "Watch the Lamb. Dave, you don't come to Mass to worship angels, you come to Mass to worship my

Son, the Lamb of God. Watch the Lamb!"

After hearing those words, I thought to myself, what am I doing! Intellectually I know that I am at Mass to worship Jesus, and yet, for years I spent my time at Mass focused on hoping to see the tornado of angels. After that Monday noon Mass, I no longer look for the tornado when at Mass. Now my focus during Mass is completely on Jesus, fully present in the Eucharist on the altar. I can honestly say, it has made the Mass much more meaningful and powerful by focusing my attention fully on Jesus.

> *"The next day he saw Jesus coming toward him and said, "Behold the Lamb of God, who takes away the sin of the world.""* (John 1:29)

Reflection question:

Jesus is the Lamb of God. What is your main focus during Mass? Is your full attention on Jesus, the Lamb of God, fully present in the Eucharist?

Has God ever pulled back the veil between heaven and earth, revealing to you in some way, the hidden reality of heaven?

Prayer:

Lamb of God,
You take away the sins of the world,
Have mercy on us.
I pray that in Your mercy,
that you will pull back the veil,
and allow us to see You for who you truly are…
The Son of God,
the Lamb of God,
who takes away the sins of the world.
Grant us peace.

Amen.

The Weight of the Sins of the World

CHAPTER 14

The Weight of the Sins of the World

ONE YEAR LATER, ON THE WEEKEND OF FEBRUARY 22ND through the 24th of 2019, we were again having our women's Christian Experience Weekend Retreat in Denmark. On Friday, February 22, 2019, at 7 p.m., just as the candidates began arriving for the retreat, I was the one processing the Blessed Sacrament in the monstrance from church over to our adoration chapel for the weekend. I was carrying the monstrance for the procession with two candle bearers in front and two behind me.

Keep in mind, I had to process the Blessed Sacrament in the monstrance from church, down the stairs to the church basement, across the church basement, down another half flight of stairs into a tunnel beneath the church driveway, over into the school basement, and then up another flight of stairs into the school and then into the former Sisters' residence to our adoration chapel. The monstrance I was carrying probably weighs three pounds at the most.

As I got as far as the church basement, the monstrance

began to get extremely heavy, to the point where my arms were shaking, and my back was aching. It literally felt like I was carrying a 200-pound body in my outstretched arms. It took every ounce of strength I had to hold the monstrance up. I was really struggling! It must have been pretty obvious how badly I was struggling to those with me because Patrick Phillips, one of the candle bearers behind me asked if I was OK and if I needed help. I told Patrick that I was OK, even though I really wasn't.

Somehow, I made it all the way over to the Adoration Chapel, but I'm not sure how. The candle bearers placed the candles on the altar, while I stood there in pain, holding the monstrance. As the candle bearers stepped away from the altar, I finally was able to place the monstrance on the altar, and immediately, all the pain in my arms and back went away! I was pretty shaken up about what had just happened, and I immediately knelt down before the Blessed Sacrament and cried!

Although the retreat that weekend was a women's retreat, I was also attending the retreat as one of two spiritual directors for the retreat. After spending a few minutes trying to pray, but mostly crying, before the Blessed Sacrament, I had to compose myself and go join the women for the start of the retreat.

On the following evening, Saturday, February 23, 2019, as part of the retreat, we were having a reconciliation service in the church. During the reconciliation service, I sat in a pew in the very back of church as the women were going to confession. I intended to wait until everyone else had gone to confession before going myself.

One of the women on the retreat, Leigh Ann Trzinski, whose husband, Deacon Jim Trzinski had just become the pastoral leader for the parishes in our linkage at the beginning of July, was sitting in a pew about halfway up in church on the far righthand side of the church. As I was praying, and preparing myself for confession, I looked up and noticed that Leigh Ann was trying to get my attention. I got up out of the pew and walked up to her. There was also another woman, Suzanne Zellner, sitting directly behind Leigh Ann. Leigh Ann asked me to sit down next to her in the pew. She then asked me to look up at the tabernacle and tell them what I saw. Just to the right of the tabernacle, and within the curtain that hangs in front of the wall behind the tabernacle, was what appeared to be the profile of a face. As I looked at the face in the curtain, it appeared to me to be the face of Jesus (see the photo in the back of the book).

As the three of us were looking at the face in awe, the face suddenly turned toward us and the mouth moved, as if talking. Leigh Ann let out a gasp and grabbed my arm so tightly that she left a bruise. The face then turned back to the profile view. All three of us acknowledged to one another that we had seen the face turn toward us, the mouth move, and then saw the face turn back to the profile view in the photo. Leigh Ann told us that she actually heard a voice, and that Jesus said to her when the mouth moved, "Don't worry, I am here with you." Leigh Ann had been struggling with some personal things and those words brought her a great deal of comfort. Suzanne Zellner and I saw the face turn, and the mouth move, but did not hear the voice. With one exception, the profile of the face remained in the curtain until February 16, 2021, when the curtain was removed for cleaning and a purple curtain was hung in its place to start the Lenten season.

During the two years that the profile of the face was visible in the curtain, our parish had quite a few people coming to our church to specifically see the face of Jesus. The funny thing about the image of the face is that when you walked right up to the tabernacle you could not see the face in the curtain at all – the face was only visible when standing at a distance of about 20 feet or more away.

On Monday, February 25, two days after first seeing the face in the curtain, and exactly one year to the day since I had seen the tornado of angels around the altar,

I had spiritual direction with Monsignor Jim Feely. We spent about an hour and a half talking about the things I had experienced over the weekend on both Friday and Saturday evenings at the Christian Experience Weekend retreat.

Although the experience of seeing the face in the curtain was not by any means discounted, as we talked our conversation began to focus much more on the events of Friday evening and the weight of the monstrance when I was processing the Blessed Sacrament over to the Adoration Chapel. As we continued to talk about the Eucharistic Procession, Father Jim asked me if I knew the story about St. Christopher. I told him that I knew he was the patron saint of travelers but I didn't really know anything else about him, so Father Jim began to tell me more about St. Christopher. He told me that Saint Christopher is believed to have lived during the third century and that he lived along a road in a small hut near a river. There was no bridge over the river. To cross the river, the people had to walk through it, but the river's current was so strong and dangerous that travelers were often swept away by the current when trying to cross the river. St. Christopher, being a very large man, made it his ministry to carry travelers across the river who otherwise would not have been able to make it across themselves.

One day he was asked by a very young boy to be carried across the river, so St. Christopher placed the young child on his shoulders and began to make his way into the river. With every step that Christopher took, the weight of the child grew heavier and heavier until he thought he wouldn't be able to make it across the river. With a great struggle, he was finally able to make it to the other side of the river. He set the boy down on the other bank and told the child that he had never carried anyone so heavy across the river. The young child then told Christopher that he was Jesus, and that Christopher had just carried the weight of the sins of the world across the river.

My spiritual director suggested that maybe what I had experienced was something similar to the experience St. Christopher had. It was at this point that Father Jim and I began to discern what God was calling me to do with these experiences. Over the next six months, this discernment became the main focus of our time spent together in spiritual direction.

Six months later, when I met with Bishop Ricken at his residence on Friday, August 30, 2019, I was telling Bishop about the experience I had with the weight of the Blessed Sacrament in the monstrance, and Bishop's first response was simply saying, "Christ bearer." Bishop Ricken then told me, "Christopher means Christ bearer, and maybe through your experience carrying the Blessed Sacrament in the monstrance, that God is calling you to be a bearer of Christ for people, to bring the message of the true presence of Christ in the Eucharist to those who don't know or those who don't believe, since there has become such a large percentage of Catholics who don't believe in the true presence of Christ in the Eucharist."

It was at this point that Bishop Ricken told me that he believed that I was being truthful with him about my experiences and encouraged me to share those experiences with people throughout the Diocese of Green Bay.

Per the bishop's encouragement, two and a half months later, I gave my first presentation on my experiences with the Blessed Sacrament. On Saturday morning, November 16, 2019, I gave a witness talk on my experience with the Eucharist at Mass and in Adoration at a Diocese of Green Bay Diaconate Community Gathering. The positive response of my witness talk by the diaconate community was overwhelming. That witness talk led to a whirlwind of invitations from parishes around the diocese over the next two and half months. Just five days after doing the witness talk for the diaconate community, I was again doing a similar presentation for an adult faith formation gathering at St. Francis of Assisi Parish in Manitowoc.

This in turn led to a talk at St. Bernard Parish in Appleton, another at All Saints in Denmark, and a talk in Stevens Point, Wisconsin, plus a number of invitations for other events, but most of them unfortunately got cancelled, due to COVID.

As I began doing presentations on my experiences with the Blessed Sacrament around the diocese, I noticed on Facebook one evening, that Sister Jackie Spaniola, the same religious sister who had taught the adult faith formation class on The Lambs Supper that my mom had taken, had posted a YouTube Video on her Facebook page. I watched the video and began to weep.

This video depicted so much of the experiences I have had in the presence of the Blessed Sacrament, including angels appearing at Mass and blood dripping into the chalice. It also showed the priest changing in appearance to Jesus at the consecration during Mass, similar to what my mom had experienced as a freshman in high school. It's a short seven-minute video titled, "The Veil Removed".

I pulled the video up on my phone as Betsy and I were about to drive to church the morning after I first saw the video. I handed my phone to Betsy and asked her to watch it while I drove us to Mass. As Betsy was watching, I turned to look at her and noticed tears were running down her cheeks. It moved her deeply and she asked me why I couldn't have waited until after Mass, so she didn't mess up her make-up. But the truth was, I wanted her to watch it before Mass, in hopes that it would place her in a better mindset for what we were about to experience when we entered the church for Mass.

Not only do I recommend watching "The Veil Removed," as it will most likely strengthen your belief in Jesus' true presence in the Eucharist, but it also ties in so beautifully to the words that Father Mark Mleziva had shared with me on the February afternoon when I experienced the tornado of angels that appeared around the altar and danced before the Lord, "Every once in a while, God will pull back the veil just a tiny bit and give us a little glimpse of heaven."

The Lord Jesus, on the night he was handed over, took bread, and, after he had given thanks, broke it and said, "This is my body that is for you. Do this in remembrance of me." (1 Corinthians 11:23-24)

Reflection questions:

Each time we receive the Eucharist at Mass, we too are carrying Jesus' body within our very bodies. We too are carrying the weight of Jesus' crucified body. When receiving the Eucharist, do you tend to just go through the motions without giving much thought to what you are participating in, or do you focus on the fact that you are receiving the true presence of Christ's body, blood, soul, and divinity?

In what ways may God be inviting you to be a bearer of Christ for people, to bring the message of the true presence of Christ in the Eucharist to those who don't understand, or those who don't believe in Christ's true presence in the Eucharist?

St. Christopher Prayer:

O Glorious St. Christopher, you have inherited a beautiful name, Christ-bearer, as a result of the wonderful legend that while carrying people across a raging stream you also carried the Child Jesus. Teach us to be true Christ-bearers to those who do not know Him. Protect all of us that travel both near and far and petition Jesus to be with us always.

Amen.

St. Christopher, pray for us!

Come Holy Spirit!

CHAPTER 15

Come Holy Spirit!

On July 1, 2018, we had a new priest, Father Paul Demuth, assigned to our linked parishes as our Sacramental Minister. Father Paul had been my homiletics teacher for the final class of my diaconate formation, so I already knew him when he arrived at our linked parishes. I really enjoyed working with Father Paul and he became a good friend during the one and a half years that he was assigned to our parishes.

Ever since I attended my very first Christian Experience Weekend retreat back in February of 2003, and due to the powerful impact that the Holy Spirit had on me that weekend and continues to have on me today, the celebration of Pentecost Sunday has taken on a whole new meaning for me. I actually get as excited to celebrate Pentecost as I get for the celebration of Christmas and Easter. Each year as we draw near to the end of the Easter Season, I begin to focus more and more on the coming of Pentecost Sunday and the outpouring of the Holy Spirit.

On June 9, 2019, Pentecost Sunday, we were celebrating our parish picnic at All Saints Parish in Denmark. Our Pentecost Sunday Mass was celebrated outside under a very large tent. The altar, ambo, and chairs for the priest, deacon, altar servers, and lector were all set up on a stage at one end of the tent. All of the music for Mass was set to polka music, and there was a polka band playing all of the music for Mass. Yes, polka Masses are a real thing at Catholic parish church picnics in Wisconsin, and they are very well attended!

Father Paul was presiding at Mass that Sunday, and I was assisting him as deacon. When the Liturgy of the Word began, the lector, Jean Vander Heyden, who was our All Saints Catholic School principal, got up and walked to the ambo to begin proclaiming the first reading. The first reading for Pentecost comes from the Acts of the Apostles, Chapter 2, verses 1-11. This is the story of the Holy Spirit descending upon all gathered in the upper room, the entire house being filled with a noise like a strong driving wind, then tongues as of fire appearing, which parted and came to rest over all present, and they were all filled with the Holy Spirit!

Father Paul and I were sitting to the righthand side of the altar as you looked up toward the stage. The ambo was to the lefthand side of the altar, and because Pentecost is the last day in the celebration of the Easter Season, the

Easter Candle was standing just to the right of the ambo. As Jean was standing at the ambo reading, from where I was sitting the Easter candle was directly between Jean and me. As I looked over toward the ambo, I had to look right through the flame of the Easter Candle to see Jean's face. The flame of the Easter Candle was literally right in the middle of the side of Jean's face.

As Jean began proclaiming the first reading about the tongues of fire, I couldn't help but notice that the flame on the Easter Candle began to slowly rotate in a clockwise motion. As the flame began rotating, I also saw small puffs of flame come off the top of the flame of the Easter Candle. The interesting thing about the puffs of flame was that they didn't just gradually disappear into the air but floated out away from the Easter Candle. Whatever direction the rotating flame happened to be leaning as the puff of flame came off the flame of the Easter Candle, that puff of flame would just continue to float off in that direction, out over the people sitting in the tent for Mass. As I looked at the tiny flames and watched them float out over the people, they appeared to me to be tongues of fire! The entire time that Jean was proclaiming the first reading, the flame on the Easter Candle continued to rotate, and the tongues of fire continued to appear off the tip of the flame and float out over the people. I was moved to tears as I watched this happen. As soon as Jean finished proclaiming the first reading, the puffs of flame stopped, and the flame on the Easter Candle stopped rotating and stood straight up.

I didn't physically see the tongues of fire rest over any individuals heads that morning, but I certainly did see them float out over top of all those in attendance. I don't know if the Holy Spirit set hearts on fire that morning, but He certainly set mine on fire.

After Mass, I asked Father Paul if he had seen the flame on the Easter Candle rotating and the tongues of fire, or little puffs of flame come off the flame of the Easter Candle and float out over the people as I had seen. He looked at me with a look of surprise and simply said no, he hadn't seen or noticed it.

The thought entered my mind: Why do I continue to see these things and no one else does? This question would continue to be a significant part of the discussion between Father Jim and me during spiritual direction.

Then there appeared to them tongues as of fire, which parted and came to rest on each one of them. And they were all filled with the Holy Spirit. (Acts 2:3-4)

Reflection question:

During the Sacrament of Confirmation, the Gifts of the Holy Spirit are poured out on us. For many of us, it takes years for the grace of those gifts of the Sacrament to manifest themselves in our life. How have you experienced the outpouring, or the manifestation of the Gifts of the Holy Spirit in your life?

Prayer:

Holy Spirit, let Your fire pour out upon us and change our hearts. Set our church and our lives on fire with the fire of Your love. Change us, renew us, sanctify us.

Amen.

You've Got to Carry That Weight

CHAPTER 16

You've Got to Carry That Weight

THE FOLLOWING WINTER, ON THE WEEKEND OF FEBRUARY 7-9, 2020, we were holding our men's Christian Experience Weekend retreat again in Denmark. On Friday, February 7, at 7:00, we again had a Eucharistic Procession to bring the Monstrance with the Blessed Sacrament from the church over to our adoration chapel for the retreat weekend. I again was carrying the monstrance and had four candle bearers processing with me – two in front of me and two behind me.

Just as had happened the previous year, as the Eucharistic procession had gotten as far as the church basement, the monstrance again began to get extremely heavy to the point where my arms were shaking and my back was aching. It again felt as though I was carrying a 200-pound body in my outstretched arms and it took every ounce of strength I had to carry the monstrance.

It was so evident that I was struggling to carry the monstrance that Curt Nelson, one of the candle bearers behind me in the procession thought for sure I was going to fall. Curt told me a bit later, "I saw you were struggling, and I was so sure you were going to fall walking up the steps from the school basement up into the school that I was planning in my head how I was going to grab the monstrance when you fell so that Jesus wouldn't fall to the floor." That comment moved me to tears then, and it still does every time I think about it now, as I think of Curt's first thought being to protect Jesus in the Blessed Sacrament.

Once again, as had happened the year before, as soon as I was able to place the monstrance on the altar in the Adoration Chapel, all the pain and discomfort I had been feeling just instantly went away. I again immediately knelt before the Blessed Sacrament to pray but could only cry as I was so moved by emotion.

Before the Eucharistic procession had even begun, the candle bearers and I were in church getting things prepared for the procession. Patrick Phillips was again going to be one of the candle bearers for the procession and as he and I were getting the candles ready for the procession, we both noticed the profile of the face in the curtain behind the tabernacle was no longer there, was no longer visible. We both were somewhat disappointed, since it had been visible for almost a full year, but we both continued with our preparations for the procession.

The next evening, Saturday, February 8, 2020, we again were celebrating the Sacrament of Reconciliation in church. As we entered the church for the reconciliation service, Patrick and I both noticed the profile of the face in the curtain behind the tabernacle was definitely gone and commented to each other about it. After both Patrick and I gone to confession that evening, and returned to our pews, we each noticed the face had suddenly reappeared on the curtain, and now with even more distinct detail! We discussed it afterwards, and were both ecstatic that the image was back, but were amazed by the fact that we both know, and had witnessed that it hadn't been there over the previous 24 hours.

The very next weekend, February 14th to the 16th, 2020, we were hosting our women's Christian Experience Weekend retreat at All Saints Parish. On Friday evening, February 14, we again had the Eucharistic Procession of the Monstrance with the Blessed Sacrament from the church over to our adoration chapel. I was literally frightened to carry the monstrance in the Eucharistic procession. I was afraid of falling and dropping the monstrance, dropping Jesus. I did not want to be the reason for Jesus falling, as he did three times during his passion. This is actually what was going through my mind. I was unable to find another deacon or priest who was available to carry the monstrance in the Friday evening procession, so I somewhat reluctantly carried the monstrance. I had four candle bearers assisting me, and there was also a group of other Christian Experience Weekend retreat Community members that joined us for the procession.

I once again, for the second time within a week, and now for the third time overall, had the exact same experience carrying the monstrance in the Eucharistic Procession. Again, the extreme weight of the monstrance caused my back and arms to ache and I struggled to be able to continue to carry the weight of the Monstrance and the Blessed Sacrament.

There was one distinct difference between this Eucharistic Procession and the previous two. When we got to the Adoration Chapel, and I was able to finally place the Monstrance with the Blessed Sacrament on the altar in the Adoration Chapel, my right shoulder continued to ache. I had a throbbing pain in my shoulder that did not immediately go away. The pain remained and lasted for about 45 minutes and then gradually just went away. The closest thing I can compare the pain in my shoulder to was the pain I felt in that same shoulder when I tore my rotator cuff 15 years before that.

After I had placed the monstrance containing the Blessed Sacrament on the altar in the Eucharistic Adoration Chapel, I again knelt before the Blessed Sacrament to pray, but instead spent about 10 minutes crying. The experience of feeling that tremendous weight of the monstrance has been extremely emotional for me, as I truly feel I am carrying the weight of Christ's body in my outstretched arms.

As I have had time to reflect and pray on these experiences, I now have a different mindset. My reflection and prayer have brought to mind the text of the Fifth Station – Simon of Cyrene helps Jesus carry the cross, from a version of the stations of the cross entitled, The Way of the Cross.

"As the strength of Jesus fails, and he is unable to proceed, the executioners seize and compel Simon of Cyrene to carry His cross. The grace of that cross changes the Cyrenean's heart and from the compulsory task, it becomes a privilege and joy."

My experience of the weight of the monstrance containing the Body of Christ, has now become for me, similar to what is described in this fifth station. Although difficult and challenging, it has become a true privilege and joy to have had these experiences.

But he was pierced for our sins, crushed for our iniquity. He bore the punishment that makes us whole, by his wounds we were healed. (Isaiah 53:53)

Reflection questions:

Do you ever reflect on or give thought to the weight of our sins that Jesus bore for our salvation?

How have your sins contributed to the suffering that Jesus bore on the cross?

If Jesus asked, would you be willing to bear some of the weight of the cross to lessen Christ's burden in some way?

Prayer:

O Lord Jesus, may it be our privilege to bear our cross. May we glory in nothing else; by the cross, may the world be crucified unto us, and we unto the world. May we never shrink from suffering but rather rejoice if we should be counted worthy to suffer for your name's sake.

Amen.

(The Way of the Cross – Fifth Station Prayer)

A Real Pandemic

CHAPTER 17

A Real Pandemic

My job title at work is architect's field representative. I am one of four field representatives working for our company. As a field representative, I am one of the people from our office that goes out onto job sites and oversees the construction, verifying that the building is being constructed per the drawings and specifications. I also attend on-site construction meetings as well as having other construction-related responsibilities. This means that I do a great deal of traveling for my job, driving from one construction job site to another. Sometimes, I am at as many as four different construction sites in a given day. This also means I have routinely put anywhere from 500 to 1,000 miles on my car in a given week.

In 2015, I began regularly driving across the state for work to Eau Claire, Wisconsin, at least once a week, more than a 220-mile drive one way. During that time, I have had many construction projects at Sacred Heart Hospital in Eau Claire, which is located right next to the University of Wisconsin-Eau Claire campus. The Hospital and University campuses actually abut each other. Beginning in 2017, I began spending nearly every Wednesday and

Thursday working in the Eau Claire area, meaning that I have spent most Wednesday nights staying overnight in a hotel in Eau Claire.

In the fall of 2019, my daughter Grace began her freshman year of college, attending the University of Wisconsin-Eau Claire. The greatest blessing of Grace going to school in Eau Claire is that I have had the opportunity to spend time with her on Wednesday evenings, which has meant taking her out to eat, taking her grocery shopping, and just spending one on one time together.

On Thursday, March 12, 2020, after I was through with all of my meetings for the day, I stopped over at Grace's dorm to pick up a bag of things from her to bring home with me. While we were in her dorm room talking, she received an email from the university saying that the following day would be the final day of in-person classes on campus, due to the COVID 19 outbreak, and the rapid spread of the virus on campus. This whole COVID 19 pandemic, which just a month earlier I wasn't really even aware of, suddenly became very real for both of us! That meant instead of taking a bag of things home for her, I was now loading as much of Grace's belongings into my car as I could fit. Betsy and I drove back over to Eau Claire on Saturday and packed up everything else up that I couldn't fit in my car on Thursday and brought Grace home.

We had planned a family vacation to the Florida Keys for the week of March 22, which was during Grace's spring break. The vacation got cancelled as Florida hotels and restaurants were closing. Within a week, Betsy and I were both asked to work from home, rather than from our offices, so we had Betsy, Grace, and me all home for an extended period of time.

The Diocese of Green Bay discontinued the obligation for in-person Mass attendance beginning on the weekend of March 15, 2020. Deacon Jim Trzinski began livestreaming our Sunday Mass via Facebook. Father Paul Demuth would celebrate Mass and Deacon Jim would assist him. I assisted Father Paul on the one weekend of the month that I was typically scheduled to preach. We would have a musician, a singer, a lector, and Deacon Jim's wife Leigh Ann livestreaming with an iPad. So, basically six people in church. Proclaiming the Gospel and preaching to an iPad was very uncomfortable.

This was an extremely difficult time for me, as I know it was for most everyone. But it wasn't the pandemic itself that was so difficult. In hindsight, the pandemic provided a great deal of blessings. I was spending all day, every day, at home with Betsy and Grace. We spent true quality time together as a family. We took the dog out for a 2½-mile walk at lunchtime every day and talked. We talked as a family so much more than we had in a long time. We spent time almost every day swimming together in our pool. We began playing board games together in the evening. It was wonderful!

What made this time so difficult for me was not being able to regularly attend Mass. I had been attending daily Mass as well as Sunday Mass. The Sunday obligation to attend Mass was so ingrained in me from childhood on that I was not at all comfortable with not attending Mass on Sunday mornings, even though I knew the obligation to do so had been removed.

The first Sunday that the obligation to attend Mass had been discontinued, Betsy, Grace and I sat in our living room and watched Mass on television as Bishop Ricken celebrated the Mass on a local station out of Green Bay. When it came to communion time, and we prayed the prayer for spiritual communion, Betsy and I cried, as we would do pretty much every Sunday going forward when watching Mass on television or livestreamed. I knew right then and there that this was going to be a very difficult time. I had such a longing to receive Jesus in the Eucharist, that it physically hurt. And I was fortunate enough to be able to receive the Eucharist every three or four weeks when I would assist and preach at Mass, unlike the majority of Catholics. Those opportunities to receive communion were amazing! I could feel my heart swelling with joy and peace as I received Jesus in the Blessed Sacrament. I truly wish that every time I receive communion, that it could feel that way!

In the fall of 2015, a group of CEW members decided to begin a program being promoted by the Green Bay Diocesan offices called "Oremus." Oremus is a prayer study program that teaches the essentials of a fruitful prayer life. We decided to meet on Wednesday mornings at 6 a.m., at All Saints Parish in Denmark. Six was a time that would allow our group to meet before heading to work and would not cut into family and other ministry time in the evenings.

Jim Gillis was one of the CEW members who would be taking part in the study program. When we made the decision on a day and time to begin the Oremus program, Jim strongly suggested that we should gather at 5 a.m. and spend an hour in Eucharistic Adoration prior to meeting for Oremus. Although some of us weren't initially excited about starting that early, we all agreed that it would be a great idea to attend adoration prior to meeting for a study program on prayer.

We began as a group of nine people gathering each Wednesday morning for one hour of Eucharistic Adoration at 5 a.m., followed by an hour and a half study program. The Oremus program was a nine-week study program, and once we completed the nine weeks, we decided that we would continue to meet each Wednesday morning, but substitute bible study for Oremus.

I have typically been the one to expose the Blessed Sacrament to begin Adoration and have also typically done Benediction at around 5:50 a.m. Over time, the number of people participating in Eucharistic Adoration on Wednesday mornings increased to about 12 to 15.

Once the pandemic began, our group did not want to discontinue Eucharistic Adoration, but due to restrictions given by the Diocese, we weren't able to do so. It was decided to begin livestreaming Wednesday morning Eucharistic Adoration via Facebook and to have a Zoom meeting for bible study after. I would be in church with one other member of our group, who would be socially distanced from me. Each week, this gave one of the members of our group the opportunity to attend Eucharistic Adoration in person. I would expose the Blessed Sacrament, and I would lead Benediction, with the other person with me responding to the prayers while we livestreamed the full hour of Eucharistic Adoration and Benediction.

What amazed me when we started livestreaming

Eucharistic Adoration is that our "attendance" jumped from around 15 up to regularly around 75, and up to as many as 115 people participating via livestream on Wednesday mornings. We had people joining us from around the country, and even one from Canada! It quickly became extremely evident that Catholics were longing for Jesus during the pandemic, both in the Eucharist and in Eucharistic Adoration.

On Sunday, May 31, 2020, Bishop Ricken allowed the faithful to receive communion in their churches, but not during Mass. We were able to have the church open for an hour after the celebration of Sunday Mass was completed for parishioners to come and receive communion. Only one person, or one family was allowed into the church at a time to receive communion. They entered through the side entrance, stood before the altar, and we prayed with them prior to receiving communion. We allowed them a short period of time for personal prayer time after receiving communion and then they exited through the main entrance. Once they had exited the church, the next person or family was allowed into church.

I was asked to distribute communion and pray with the individuals and families that came to receive the Eucharist, while Deacon Jim was at the church entrance allowing people to enter and to control social distancing. The thing that surprised me the most, although it probably shouldn't have, was the level of reverence everyone had as they entered church to receive communion. As I gave people communion for the first time in over two months, nearly everyone who came to church that initial Sunday morning either had tears welling up in their eyes or were outright sobbing as they received the Eucharist! It was Beautiful!

For me it was an experience of complete joy and complete sorrow all at the same time. Joy that they were getting the opportunity to receive Jesus in the Blessed Sacrament and were so emotional in doing so, and sorrow in that they, and so many others had been deprived of the one thing that we as Catholics should long for more than anything in lives.

God was showing me in a beautifully new and very profound way that His son Jesus is truly present in the Eucharist, and even though so many Catholics do not believe in the true presence of Jesus in the Eucharist, those who do are being deeply blessed by it.

As a member of the Diocese of Green Bay Diocesan Pastoral Council, at our council meeting on Saturday, April 2, 2022, Bishop David Ricken announced to the council that after having gone through the COVID 19 pandemic, and from the input he had received from so many people around the diocese regarding not being able to receive Jesus in the Eucharist, that he will never again close the churches. To which the entire council applauded him.

As someone who suffers from the effects of long-haul COVID symptoms, I have spent quite a bit of time reflecting back on what many have called "The Lost Year of 2020." I in no way mean any disrespect toward those who have lost their lives, or have lost loved ones due to COVID 19, but I really have to question what the bigger pandemic was? Was it the virus that swept over our world causing death and health issues for millions of people or was it the loss of gathering as community for 2.6 billion Christians worldwide, and the loss of Jesus in the Eucharist, and in Eucharistic Adoration, for over a billion Catholics worldwide during the pandemic shutdown? I believe they all have negatively affected our world tremendously.

O God, you are my God, for you I long! For you my soul is thirsting. My body pines for you like a dry weary land without water. I look to you in the sanctuary to see your power and glory. (Psalm 63:2-3)

Reflection questions:

Have you ever longed for the presence of God in your life?

Have you ever longed to receive Jesus in the Eucharist?

How did the pandemic affect your spiritual life? Did you grow in faith, or struggle to remain close to God?

Prayer:

Lord Jesus, Our deepest longing is for You, and it is only in you that we will ever be satisfied. May our longing for you, and your Holy presence in the Eucharist, be satisfied through our participation in Holy Communion, and in Eucharistic Adoration, as that is where we are able to experience You most intimately. Fill the emptiness of our hearts through Your presence in the Eucharist.

Amen.

Bringing the Heat

CHAPTER 18

Bringing the Heat

On New Year's Day 2021, the Solemnity of Mary, Mother of God, I served as deacon at Mass. This would be the last Mass I served as deacon with Father Paul Demuth presiding. Father Paul had been re-assigned to serve as sacramental minister at another parish in the diocese. Mass that morning was being celebrated at All Saints Parish in Denmark.

During Mass, as the Eucharistic prayer began, I was standing to the righthand side of Father Paul. At the epiclesis, which is the part of the Eucharistic Prayer where the priest extends his hands over the bread and wine and prays, asking God the Father to send down the Holy Spirit in order to sanctify the offerings so that they may become the Body and Blood of Jesus, the deacon kneels, and remains kneeling for the consecration of the bread and wine.

At the epiclesis, I knelt, and as I was kneeling, and Father Paul was praying the prayers of consecration, I was very intently watching first the host, and then the Chalice, as Father elevated each of them. I have been doing this consistently at every Mass, ever since I heard that voice at daily Mass say, "Dave, watch the Lamb!"

At the moment when Father Paul elevated the chalice, I saw continuous, intense heat waves rising up out of the top of the Chalice. It looked similar to the heat waves you see above a very hot fire! The heat waves were so intense, and appeared to be so hot, that they rose all the way up to the ceiling of the sanctuary! As I watched this happen, I was immediately moved to tears. Father Paul kept the chalice elevated for about five or six seconds, and as he lowered the chalice and placed it back on the corporal on the altar, the heat waves suddenly stopped! As I stood for the proclamation of the mystery of faith, I continued to cry through the remainder of the Eucharistic Prayer. I also continued to have tears welling up in my eyes as I was distributing communion.

One year later, on Sunday, January 2, 2022, I was again assisting as deacon at Mass at All Saints Parish in Denmark. This time, Father Xavier Amirtham, O. Praem., the pastor assigned to our linked parishes 11 ½ months earlier, was presiding at Mass. Again, at the consecration, as Father Xavier elevated the chalice, I saw continuous, intense heat waves rising up out of the top of the Chalice, just as I had seen a year earlier! Again, the heat waves rose up to the ceiling of the sanctuary! As I watched this happen, I was again moved to tears.

After having had these experiences, and mentioning them during witness talks, I have had five other people mention to me that they too have seen heat waves rising from either the Host, the chalice, or both during Mass. I find it reassuring that this is an experience that others have also had during Mass.

I have had many other emotional experiences during Mass, Eucharistic Adoration, or when presiding at a Liturgy of the Word with Communion Service, where I am in the presence of the Blessed Sacrament and I have just started to cry for what sometimes seems like no apparent reason. I spoke to Monsignor Jim Feely, my spiritual director, about this on a number of occasions, and he has told me that it sounds to him like I have been blessed with the gift of tears – specifically the gift of tears when in the presence of the Blessed Sacrament.

I hadn't ever heard of the gift of tears before Father Jim mentioned it, but his explanation makes a great deal of sense to me, as I have no other way to explain the depth of emotion I experience so often in the presence of the Eucharist and when experiencing these amazing glimpses of heaven on earth.

For our God is a consuming fire.
(Hebrews 12:29)

Reflection questions:

How have you experienced our Lord as a consuming fire in your life?

Does the thought of, or participation in, the Eucharist set your heart on fire?

Prayer:

Lord Jesus, I pray that I may experience your consuming fire in the Eucharist. May my reception of the Eucharist and my participation in Eucharistic Adoration set my heart on fire. Through Your grace, may that fire within my heart be used to set other hearts on fire for the Eucharist.

Amen.

More Tears

CHAPTER 19

More Tears

Due to the COVID 19 pandemic, our Denmark Area Christian Experience Weekend retreat core group made the difficult decision to cancel our annual men's and women's retreats that were scheduled for February of 2021. Because of the profound impact the retreats have had on me, the cancellation of the retreats hit me pretty hard.

For the previous 10 years, our Denmark Area Christian Experience Weekends had been my passion and something that I would look forward to the entire year. The gathering as a community, the gathering as men's and women's teams to plan the retreats, an entire community of people working together to do the Lord's work, always raised the level of excitement and anticipation within me. But what I had always looked forward to the most was experiencing lives being changed and transformed by the power and presence of the Holy Spirit over the course of a weekend. That would not happen in February 2021, and it was very difficult for me. It was almost heartbreaking.

When we made the decision to cancel our retreat weekends, we also decided that if things appeared to be clearing up with COVID 19 during the summer, we would consider holding our retreats in the fall of 2021. As things did improve considerably during the summer, we decided to hold a meeting of our Christian Experience Weekend core group on June 21, 2021, and moved forward with plans to hold retreats in October. Our women's retreat was scheduled for the weekend of October 22, 23 and 24, 2021, and our men's weekend was scheduled for October 29, 30 and 31, 2021. My sister Marie agreed to be the women's rector, and I volunteered to be the men's rector.

On September 19, 2021, we held our first men's and women's team meetings. As soon as we began meeting as men's and women's teams and began planning the retreats, I felt there was a strong spiritual attack taking place.

Since I first began having spiritual experiences in the presence of the Blessed Sacrament at Mass and in Eucharistic Adoration, I have experienced a great deal of spiritual attack from Satan. Since we first began holding Christian Experience Weekend retreats in Denmark, I have also experienced spiritual attack. It seems Satan works very hard to derail the things that have the most spiritual impact and renewal. Trying to plan our fall of 2021 retreats was no different.

On October 10, following our third men's and women's team meetings, there was a great deal of concern raised over the rise in COVID 19 cases in our area. There were very strong feelings for holding the weekends and very strong feelings as to why we shouldn't. After a lengthy discussion, we decided to have all the members of our men's and women's teams vote as to whether they felt we should go ahead with our retreats as planned.

On Sunday, October 17, prior to our team meetings, everyone had an opportunity to discuss their point of view, and we then voted. The results of the vote were to not hold our women's weekend, but there was overwhelmingly large support to hold our men's retreat, which we did.

On Friday evening, October 29, 2021, we began our first Denmark Area Christian Experience Weekend retreat in 19 months. We again set up our adoration chapel and had a Eucharistic procession from the church over to the Adoration Chapel on Friday evening. Because I was the rector for the retreat, and had other responsibilities, one of which was to be available to the retreat candidates as they arrived for the weekend, I instead asked Father Christin Raj, O. Praem., the priest who celebrated our team liturgy prior to the candidates arriving for the retreat, if he would like to process the Blessed Sacrament over to the Adoration Chapel for us. Father Christin happily agreed.

I was in the church basement as Father Christin processed the Blessed Sacrament through on his way to the chapel. As he and the candle bearers processed through, and I stood there in the presence of the Blessed Sacrament, I immediately broke down in tears, tears of absolute joy, to be again hosting our men's retreat weekend, but even more so, complete joy to be in Christ's presence! Knowing that Christ would again be present in our Adoration Chapel for the entire weekend, gave me a sense of peace that everything was going to be fine. And it was fine! It was an amazing retreat weekend. The Holy Spirit was so powerfully present! It was very evident that those who attended really needed the retreat and needed to experience Christian Community that had been missing from our lives over the past two years.

I prayed at the conclusion of the retreat that we would never again have to wait two years to gather as a Christian Experience Weekend community, as spiritual renewal is so desperately needed in our world today.

Let us be concerned for one another, to help one another to show love and to do good. Let us not give up the habit of meeting together, as some are doing. Instead, let us encourage one another all the more, since you see that the Day of the Lord is coming nearer.
(Hebrews 10:24-25)

Reflection questions:

In what way has a Christian community had a profound impact on your life?

Have you sought out a Christian community or group to be spiritually fed, or to help feed others?

Have you felt that there is something missing in your spiritual life? Pray and reflect on where God may be leading you.

Prayer:

Loving Lord, Feed the spiritual hunger in our lives, and through Your Holy Spirit, draw us to groups and communities of likeminded Christian people. Renew in us a passion for our faith, and a desire to share our faith with others who are spiritually hungry. We ask this through Christ our Lord.

Amen.

The Holy Spirit is Alive!

CHAPTER 20

The Holy Spirit is Alive!

In February of 2022, we again held both our annual men's and women's Christian Experience Weekend retreats in Denmark. On the weekend of February 18-20 we held our men's retreat, and on the weekend of February 25-27 we held our women's retreat. Because of COVID 19 having cancelled and shut so many things down, it was very obvious that people were longing for spiritual renewal in their lives, and we had a great turnout for both weekends.

My role for the women's retreat weekend was to be the spiritual director. On Friday evening, February 25, 2022, for the first time in 24 months, I again processed the Blessed Sacrament from church over to our Eucharistic Adoration Chapel as our women's retreat weekend was about to begin. I can honestly say that I again had concerns over being the one carrying the Blessed Sacrament for the Eucharistic Procession. I was concerned if I would again experience the extreme weight and if I would be able to actually make it the entire procession.

My concerns became reality. As we processed as far as the church basement while carrying the Blessed Sacrament in the monstrance, I again had the same experience. As had happened the previous three times I had carried the Blessed Sacrament in the Eucharistic procession, the weight of the monstrance caused my back and arms to ache and I again struggled carrying the weight of the Monstrance and the Blessed Sacrament. As I got to about halfway point of the procession, I began to get muscle spasms in the lower lefthand side of my back which continued for the rest of the procession.

I again did manage to make it all the way to the Adoration Chapel with the Blessed Sacrament, but when I placed the monstrance on the altar, the muscle spasms in my back continued. I again knelt before the Blessed Sacrament and wept. I also said a prayer of thanksgiving to God for allowing me to suffer in this manner for Christ, and I offered up the pain I was experiencing for the women who would be on the retreat with me.

There were quite a few people in the chapel, and as I struggled to get up to leave, people came to me and hugged me, knowing that I had again felt the incredible weight of carrying the Body of Christ. It wasn't just me that got emotional in the chapel this time. I walked down the hall toward the library of the school, where the women were gathering to begin the retreat, and the muscle spasms continued, and were actually strong enough that they were taking my breath away.

Betsy had been working at the registration table in the corridor just outside of the library, checking the retreatants in. As I walked up to her, she noticed I had tears in my eyes. She asked me if everything was all right, and I told her I had the same experience carrying the Blessed Sacrament in the monstrance, and that I was now having pretty intense muscle spasms in my back. She gave me some extra strength Tylenol in hopes it would take the edge off the back pain I was experiencing. I went into the retreat conference room for the start of the women's retreat, and it took nearly an hour for the muscle spasms to start to die down and eventually go away. This was by far the most intense pain I had felt while carrying the Blessed Sacrament in the monstrance.

Many different people are asked to do the talks on a Christian Experience Weekend retreat, including priests, deacons, religious sisters, and laypeople. For this particular retreat weekend, Bishop David Ricken was asked to do a talk on Grace on Saturday afternoon Feb. 26, 2022.

As I have mentioned prior, the presence and fire of the Holy Spirit is so evident on Christian Experience Weekend retreats. On Saturday afternoon, I was watching for Bishop Ricken to arrive to do his talk. When he arrived, I met him at the door and walked him to our Adoration Chapel for some prayer time before his talk. There were also members of our community in the chapel to pray with Bishop Ricken and pray for him before his talk, as well as while he was doing his talk.

As Bishop Ricken and I walked down the hall to the Adoration Chapel, Bishop suddenly stopped, looked at me and said, "Do you feel that? The Holy Spirit is here! The Holy Spirit is filling this place!" My thought was, of course He's here, He's always here on these weekends. But what transpired with the presence of the Holy Spirit over the next hour was even beyond anything I had experienced on a Christian Experience Weekend before.

We got to the Adoration Chapel, and Bishop Ricken knelt before the Blessed Sacrament and prayed silently for about five minutes. Then, before I walked him down to the school library, where he would do his talk, all those in the Adoration Chapel, rose, laid hands on our bishop, and prayed over him, and then I had the honor of giving him a blessing. It was an amazingly humbling experience to pray a blessing over Bishop Ricken, a man I have so much respect and admiration for.

We walked down to the retreat conference room, where Bishop Ricken gave his talk on Grace, and was grace ever poured out on us in that room who witnessed his talk! At the conclusion of the bishop's talk, he paused, and he began to pray. The prayer was not something that he had written in his notes, or something that seemed planned, he just simply began to pray from the very depths of his heart, and the prayer was so powerful that I began to cry. His prayer brought me to a deeply spiritual realm that I have rarely felt in my life.

As I looked around the room, the face of every woman I could see in that room had tears rolling down their cheeks. Bishop Ricken literally moved the entire room of about 35 people to tears with a beautiful and powerful prayer! As he concluded his prayer and talk, I was sitting next to Suzanne Zellner, and we both just looked at each other with eyes filled with tears, and said simultaneously, "Wow!"

I had the honor of walking Bishop Ricken back to the Adoration Chapel following his talk. As we were walking down the hallway, Bishop again stopped and looked at me and said, "I don't know what happened back there. I didn't plan that prayer. The Holy Spirit just got hold of me and took over!" Yes, He did!

When Bishop Ricken and I got back to the Adoration

Chapel, he again knelt before the Blessed Sacrament and silently prayed for a few minutes. As he rose, all of us who were in the chapel again prayed a prayer of thanksgiving over him.

As Bishop was preparing to leave, the next speaker, Eileen Gale, entered the room. She and Bishop Ricken are friends, and when he saw her, he asked if he could pray a prayer of blessing over her. As Bishop Ricken laid his hands on the head of Eileen, he began praying in tongues over her. I could not understand a word of what he prayed, but me and everyone else in the room broke down in tears and felt this unbelievable joy fill our hearts. I was again brought to a deeply spiritual realm similar to what I had felt following Bishop's prayer at the conclusion of his talk.

Betsy was over in church at All Saints for the 4 p.m. Vigil Mass, and she told me later that after Bishop Ricken had left the chapel, he went straight over to church. He was so on fire with the Holy Spirit that he asked our priest, Father Xavier Amirtham, if he could speak to the congregation before Mass. Betsy said that the bishop came out to the ambo and began speaking and it was so amazing, powerful, and emotional! She said it was apparent that he was filled with the Holy Spirit, and that she too felt the power of the Holy Spirit there in church as Bishop Ricken spoke!

Patrick Phillips was one of the people in the Adoration Chapel when Bishop Ricken prayed in tongues over Eileen Gale. I was talking with him and a few of the women who were in both the library and the Adoration Chapel, about the feeling we had experienced when Bishop began praying to conclude his talk and the same feeling that we experienced when he began praying in tongues. Patrick said that he imagines what we felt was similar to the description of spiritual ecstasy he had heard and read about. After he described it that way, that is the only description that I think comes even close to explaining what I personally had experienced.

That same evening, after the retreat activities had concluded for the evening, I went into the Adoration Chapel to pray before the Blessed Sacrament for a while before going home to get some sleep. Suzanne Zellner was also in the chapel with me. Suzanne was sitting toward the back righthand corner of the chapel. I knelt on a kneeler in front and slightly to the left of the monstrance, maybe about four feet away from the monstrance. As I was looking at the Blessed Sacrament in the monstrance as I prayed, I could swear the host was bleeding. It appeared that at the center of the host, blood began forming on the surface of the host. The spot that appeared to be bleeding was about the size of a quarter. I began to get emotional.

I stood up and walked right up to the monstrance and looked very closely at the host, but when I got up close to the host, it looked normal, and not as if it were bleeding at all. Suzanne asked me what was wrong, and I told her that I could have sworn that the host was bleeding.

I went back and knelt at the kneeler, and as I looked up at the monstrance, the host again looked like blood was forming on the surface of the center of the host. I knelt there and watched it for a while as I prayed. I again became emotional. As I finished praying and got up to leave, I again walked up to the monstrance to get a closer look. Again, up close it looked like a normal host and did not appear to be bleeding. I was dumbfounded that there was no blood, but yet each time I knelt before the Blessed Sacrament, it absolutely appeared to be bleeding.

I wasn't sure what to make of what I had just experienced, but thanked God for allowing me to see the bleeding host, if even for just short periods of time. I also thanked Him for allowing me, through Bishop Ricken, to experience the Holy Spirit so profoundly throughout that day!

Then they said to each other, "Were not our hearts burning within us while he spoke to us..."?
(Luke 24:32)

Reflection questions:

Have you ever had a spiritual experience where you broke down in tears, or felt an unbelievable joy fill your heart?

In what ways have you experienced your heart burning within you when hearing someone speak, or pray?

In what ways can we prepare our hearts to experience the presence of the Holy Spirit in a profound way?

Prayer:

Heavenly Father, open my heart to recognize Your presence in my life. It is my deepest desire and prayer to be set on fire by You! May I experience the pure joy of my heart burning within me in Your presence. May the burning of my heart never be extinguished. I ask this through Jesus Christ, my Lord.

Amen.

Corpus Christi

CHAPTER 21

Corpus Christi

Since reading Scott Hahn's book, *The Lamb's Supper*, the Solemnity of Corpus Christi is one of the feast days in the Church's liturgical year that I most look forward to. I always look forward with excitement to hearing the readings that focus on the Eucharist, as well as hearing the homily, anticipating hearing about Eucharistic miracles, or some reference to the Eucharist being the source and summit of our faith – just anything to help the faithful get excited about the Eucharist and the Eucharistic Liturgy. I also pray that this Solemnity will help the faithful to fully believe in the true presence of Christ in the Blessed Sacrament. Unfortunately, I have frequently been disappointed. I have attended Mass on the Solemnity of Corpus Christi in numerous churches around the state of Wisconsin, as well as in Montana, and more often than not, the priest or deacon doesn't even mention the Eucharist in their homilies.

On Memorial Day weekend of 2016, I moved my son, John, out to Big Sky, MT, where he was going to begin a new job. That weekend, on Sunday, May 29, 2016, I attended Mass in a small town in Montana, for the celebration of the Solemnity of Corpus Christi. Not only did the priest not mention the Eucharist in a homily but spent 45 minutes preaching a sermon on why the Catholic Church should go back to the pre-Vatican II celebration of the Mass in Latin with the priest facing away from the congregation. Boy, was that sermon a disappointment to hear on the Solemnity of Corpus Christi!

On June 19, 2022, the Solemnity of Corpus Christi, the Diocese of Green Bay kicked off a three-year Eucharistic Revival, just as every other diocese in the United States did. The Solemnity of Corpus Christi was celebrated, and the three-year Eucharistic Revival was begun with a Eucharistic Procession from cathedrals in every diocese of the United States.

In the Diocese of Green Bay, Bishop David Ricken celebrated 9 a.m. Sunday Mass at St. Francis Xavier Cathedral in downtown Green Bay. Immediately following Mass, Bishop Ricken led a 1.2-mile Eucharistic Procession from the Cathedral to St. Mary of the Angels Parish in Green Bay.

I attended the 9 a.m. Sunday Mass at St. Francis Xavier Cathedral on the Solemnity of Corpus Christi. This was one Mass where the homily did not disappoint!

Bishop Ricken was absolutely on fire with the Holy Spirit as he preached passionately about the Eucharist and the Eucharistic Revival that we were beginning in the diocese and around the country! It was so passionate and so emotional that I cried through most of Bishop's homily! I was also moved to tears during the Eucharistic Prayer, as well as when I received Holy Communion. I again was experiencing a deeply spiritual realm similar to that which I experienced at the bishop's talk at CEW in February. The Holy Spirit had definitely worked through Bishop Ricken to set my heart to burning!

Immediately following Mass, the Blessed Sacrament was exposed on the altar and a short period of silent prayer took place. Then, the Eucharistic Procession began and it was beautiful! Bishop Ricken took the monstrance from the altar and began the procession down the main aisle to the front doors of the Cathedral. Bishop was led by a cross bearer and two candle bearers. Directly behind them were all of the children who had made their First Holy Communion in the spring from the Cathedral parish. They each carried a basket filled with rose petals and dropped rose petals ahead of the Blessed Sacrament throughout the entire procession. Directly following the First Communicants were a group of men from the Knights of Columbus in their full liturgical attire. Immediately following the Knights was Bishop Ricken, carrying the Blessed Sacrament in the monstrance. As Bishop Ricken processed down the aisle, the people in the pews, including me, began to exit into the main aisle and follow the bishop and Jesus in the monstrance in procession. As Bishop Ricken got to the front doors of the cathedral, there were four men, each bearing a corner pole supporting the canopy that the monstrance with the Blessed Sacrament would remain under throughout the procession.

As the procession silently began moving east down Doty Street, away from the Cathedral, the one thing I immediately noticed was that there were so many birds singing as we were walking. I work only five blocks from the cathedral, and I can honestly say that I have never heard as many birds singing in downtown Green Bay as there were that Sunday morning. It was as if the birds were singing their praises to Jesus as he was processed down the street past them.

When we got to the first intersection a block to the east of the cathedral, I looked back and there were people about eight wide walking down the lefthand side of the street and the procession extended at least one full city block long. The procession basically took up half the width of the street. I was simply amazed at the large number of people who were processing. Men and women of all ages, entire families, and I was really surprised at the number of children taking part in the procession, from very young through high school aged.

After walking about two blocks, a lady somewhere behind me in the group began praying the Rosary, and everyone joined in! It was so beautiful to be part of such a large group of people, who had moments earlier been completely silent in the presence of Jesus in the blessed Sacrament and were now praying the Rosary in unison!

It seemed like from the moment we began praying the Rosary, there were suddenly people watching out of their windows, there were people coming out of their front doors, out onto their front porches, and out into their yards to watch the Eucharistic Procession pass their homes. The vast majority of those who came out of their homes, immediately signed themselves with the sign of the cross, and began to join in praying the Rosary. There were children who began walking down the sidewalk alongside of the procession until we reached the end of their block. There were cars that were stopped at the intersections as we processed past them, and many of the people in the cars also signed themselves and began praying the Rosary along with us. As I watched the people come out of their homes and participate in the procession or the prayers, I again was moved to tears of utter joy!

As we got to about the halfway point to St. Mary of the Angels Parish, Father Brian Belongia, the pastor at St. Francis Xavier Cathedral Parish, who had concelebrated the Mass with Bishop Ricken, took over for the bishop in carrying Jesus in the monstrance. From this point on, Bishop Ricken walked with his crozier out ahead of the canopy with the monstrance beneath it, leading the procession.

The procession had now turned south on Irwin Street and was heading straight toward St. Mary of the Angels Parish. When we got to and crossed Mason Street, one of the busiest streets in Green Bay, I was amazed at the respect of the drivers who had to sit at the intersection of Irwin and Mason Streets as an entire block long procession of people made their way across the intersection. Nobody honked their horn or seemed in any way impatient waiting for us. It was such a peaceful walk.

As we arrived at St. Mary of the Angels Parish and entered the church, Father Brian placed the monstrance with the Blessed Sacrament on the altar as the procession filed into church and into the pews. We were given some brief time for silent prayer before the Blessed Sacrament and I prayed a prayer of thanksgiving for the beautiful and amazing experience that I was blessed to participate in that morning.

After the brief period of prayer time, Bishop Ricken then led us in Benediction. As we began the prayers and songs of Benediction, I was again moved to tears in the presence of Jesus in the Blessed Sacrament. The tears were again tears of complete joy that I continue to feel when I am in the presence of Jesus, fully present in the Blessed Sacrament.

After the Blessed Sacrament was reposed in the tabernacle, and people began to leave the church, this amazing sense of peace came over me and my heart was filled with pure joy. I can't even put into words how amazing it felt to be part of this celebration. This was, by far, the most amazing, powerful Solemnity of Corpus Christi celebration I had ever experienced! It honestly felt like all those disappointing experiences I previously had had on past Solemnities of Corpus Christi were more than made up for with my experience that morning. Thank you, Jesus!

The cup of blessing that we bless, is it not a participation in the blood of Christ? The bread that we break, is it not a participation in the body of Christ? (1 Corinthians 10:16)

Reflection questions:

How does the Eucharist nourish and enrich your life?

In what ways can you share the gift of life you receive in the Eucharist with those in need?

Prayer:

Jesus, my Lord and my God, Thank you for the gift of the Holy Eucharist. It is in the Eucharist that we experience what self-sacrificing love is. It is in the Blessed Sacrament that we are united as one body, the Body of Christ. As you draw us to yourself in Holy Communion, may we in turn draw others to you in the Eucharist, as Your living, breathing, walking, talking tabernacles. May we share You, the greatest gift we have been given, with our brothers and sisters in Christ.

Amen.

Prayer and Fasting

CHAPTER 22

Prayer and Fasting

On the weekend of February 17, 18, and 19, 2023, I again participated in our Denmark Area CEW Men's retreat weekend, serving as the retreat spiritual director. As is typical at CEW, on Saturday evening, February 18, we celebrated the Sacrament of Reconciliation which includes a reconciliation service.

I went to confession that evening to Father Christin Raj, O. Praem. Father Christin has become a very good friend since he arrived as pastor at Holy Cross Parish in Mishicot. Back in November of 2021, I had given a presentation at Holy Cross Parish on my experiences in the presence of the Eucharist. Father Christin, as pastor of Holy Cross, was in attendance for my presentation, and therefore is well aware of the experiences that I have had.

After confessing my sins and receiving absolution, I was getting up out of the chair to leave and go back to my pew to do my penance. Father Christin suddenly said, "Wait! There is something I need to tell you. The Lord has put it on my heart that I need to tell you that He wants you to pray harder, and fast more, because he wants to show you more visions."

I agreed that I would pray more intently and fast more, but I also teared up. Father Christin's words made my heart skip a little bit with joy, and yet at the same time his words actually scared me. I think the fear comes from the fact I have come to realize that as amazing as these experiences have been, there is also great responsibility that goes along with the experiences I have been having. Needless to say, I went back to the pew and prayed very intently as tears streamed down my cheeks.

On Sunday morning of the retreat weekend, each of the table groups go to individual rooms in the school building for what is referred to as a table chapel. In each room there is a table, surrounded by chairs – one for each of the individuals in that table group. On the table, there is a crucifix, a bible, and a lit candle. This is time to spend about an hour in prayer with the group of people you have sat at a table and formed a small Christian community with throughout the weekend.

I was part of the team table group, and as is typical, the team table chapel was in the Eucharistic Chapel that we set up for the retreat weekend. Therefore, our table group had the opportunity to pray before Jesus in the Blessed

Sacrament, exposed in the Monstrance on the altar. As the retreat team entered the Eucharistic Chapel, our CEW members who had been in adoration in the Eucharistic Chapel left to give us privacy, and then returned when the team table group finished their table chapel time.

As we were completing our group prayer time, Deacon Conrad Kieltyka, who was an assistant rector on the weekend, was part of our team table group. Deacon Conrad put on the humeral veil and went to the altar and picked up the monstrance. He walked up to each of the men in the chapel, and held Jesus in the monstrance right in front of each of us individually. He held the monstrance before us for a minute or so, and then blessed us with the Blessed Sacrament. As Deacon Conrad held the monstrance about 18 inches in front of my face, I was overcome by emotion, and began sobbing. All I could think about was Father Christin's words to me the night before at Reconciliation, that I needed to pray harder and fast more because the Lord wants to show me more visions. Over the next couple weeks, I prayed intently about what Father Christin had said to me and I fasted.

Two weeks after our men's CEW retreat, we held our Denmark Area CEW women's retreat weekend. I again served as the spiritual director for the retreat weekend.

On Sunday morning, March 5, 2023, we again had our table chapels. Just as had been done on the men's retreat two weeks earlier, the team table group gathered for our table chapel in the Eucharistic Chapel we had set up for the retreat weekend. The prayer time spent with the women on team was very emotional, and a great deal of petitions and pain were revealed through our time in prayer.

As we were concluding our table chapel, I decided to do as Deacon Conrad had done two weeks prior on our men's CEW. I vested in my alb and stole, as well as the humeral veil, which I had left in the adjoining closet after I had processed the Blessed Sacrament over to the Eucharistic Chapel on Friday evening. As a side note, Friday evening had been the first time since February 2019, and the first time in the past five times of processing the Blessed Sacrament to the Eucharistic Chapel, that I didn't experience the extreme weight of the monstrance.

As Deacon Conrad had done, after vesting, I walked over to the altar, and placing my hands into the inside pockets of the humeral veil, I lifted the monstrance from the altar, and walked up individually to each of the women, who were sitting in a large circle, and held Jesus in the monstrance in front of each of them. I held the monstrance in front of each one of them for approximately two minutes, did a blessing over them with the Blessed Sacrament, and moved on to the next person.

As I began doing this, something happened that I had never before experienced, and is extremely difficult to describe in words. As I held the Blessed Sacrament in the monstrance before each of the women, whatever pain they were experiencing, whatever was on their heart as they looked upon Jesus in the Blessed Sacrament, was somehow, mystically placed by God into my heart. I physically felt their pain and knew what was on their heart. As each of the women began crying as I held Jesus before them, I too cried with them and for them as I experienced their pain and sorrow right along with them.

After I had held Jesus before them and blessed each of them with the Blessed Sacrament, I could not stop crying. I was overwhelmed with what I had experienced and was continuing to feel in my heart. There was an unbelievable empathy that I was feeling for each one of them.

As we concluded, and the women began heading back to the conference room to gather with the rest of the women on the retreat, one of the women, my very dear friend, Karen Coppersmith, came up to me in the chapel and was still crying. She gave me a big hug, and said to me, "As you held the Blessed Sacrament in front of me, the host began beating like a living heart." Karen was shaking, and couldn't stop crying.

Another of the ladies, Valerie Martin, also stayed back in the chapel to talk to me. Valerie said, "As I looked at the monstrance, I couldn't see your face. The monstrance completely covered your face, but I could see your tears falling from behind the monstrance. I had this vision that they were the tears of Christ, and he was right there crying with me."

After taking off the vestments, I also returned to the conference room, just in time for the meal prayer before lunch. As the women left the conference room to go down to the dining hall, I stayed back and continued to cry. I was an absolute emotional wreck after what I had just experienced.

Three of the ladies remained behind – Eileen Gale, who was the retreat rector, Emily LeGreve, who was her assistant rector, and Valerie Martin who provided the music for our Masses and prayer services for the retreat. Eileen noticed I was crying, and asked if everything was OK. All three of them walked over to me, and I did my best to describe to them what I had just experienced in the Eucharistic Chapel.

Eileen asked if they could pray over me, which I emphatically said, "Yes!" Emily and Valerie laid hands on me, and Eileen put her arm around me as she began praying. She prayed a prayer of thanksgiving, and a prayer of blessing over me. She also invoked the intercession of St. John Bosco. This amazing sense of peace came over me as the three of them prayed over me and blessed me.

After Eileen had finished praying, she said with a smile on her face, "I could feel your heart beating as I prayed." After a few seconds, Eileen looked back at me with a kind of a puzzled look on her face and said, "I have no idea why I asked for the intercession of St. John Bosco. I don't think I have ever prayed and asked for his intercession before in my life! I don't know what that was all about." I looked at Eileen, smiled, and said, "I know why." I then explained to her the experience I had at St. John Bosco Youth Day at Holy Hill in October 2013. I told her about the prayer I prayed when I saw the two teenage boys fall to their knees, and then flat on their faces sobbing, when being blessed by Jesus in the Blessed Sacrament. I explained how I asked God to be give me the grace of having the same passion for the Eucharist that those two young men had, and how it was after praying that prayer, that I began having experiences in the presence of the Blessed Sacrament.

The following morning, Monday, March 6, 2023, during my morning prayer time, I was reading a daily reflection from the book, The Wisdom of Fulton Sheen – 365

Days of Inspiration, and the quote/reflection for the day was, "A person is merciful when he feels the sorrow and misery of another as if it were his own." As I sat there in prayer, reflecting on this quote from Bishop Fulton Sheen, I thought to myself, I think that might describe what I experienced yesterday in the Eucharistic Chapel!

Each morning during my morning prayers, I read the readings for Mass for that day, and spend time reflecting on them. One of the ways I reflect on the readings is by watching a short online daily reflection video from Dr. Tim Gray on the FORMED.org platform. Dr. Gray's video this particular morning spoke about how we need to remember that we are all in the church together. What happens to the church, happens to all the members of the church. This led me to reflect on the scripture passages from 1 Corinthians, Chapter 12, verses 12, 14, and 26. "As a body is one though it has many parts, and all the parts of the body, though many, are one body, so also Christ. Now the body is not a single part, but many. If one part suffers, all the parts suffer with it."

As I reflected on this scripture, and Bishop Fulton Sheen's quote, I couldn't help but feel that God was speaking directly to my heart about my experiences the day before. I hurt because the women I was with were hurting. I suffered because they were suffering. I feel that God is calling me, and helping me to grow in mercy, compassion, and empathy for others, and he is using the Blessed Sacrament, and Christ's own suffering to help me understand this. I literally sat on my couch that Monday morning and cried for an hour and a half as I prayed.

As I was driving to a meeting at St. Vincent Hospital in Green Bay for work that morning, I received a text from Eileen Gale, but didn't read it until I arrived in the parking ramp at St. Vincent Hospital.

Eileen was so excited and told me that her prayers were so full and rich that morning. She thanked me for doing the blessing with Jesus in the monstrance.

I, in turn, shared with Eileen my morning prayer experience while reading the reflection from Bishop Fulton Sheen, and from the reflection on FORMED that got me reflecting on us being all one body, and when one part of the body suffers, the entire body suffers. I told Eileen, "I feel Christ showed me what it means to suffer for the Body of Christ." I then thanked her for facilitating one of the best weekends of my life!

Eileen's response back floored me, as she said, "Thank you for trusting me enough to share these very REAL experiences of the Lord. I LOVE how He is working in and through you. You are called to such incredible work, and He loves YOU and trusts YOU with His heart and His children's as well. Thank you for saying YES to this mission that lies before you. Like Blessed Mother whose heart was pierced so she could participate in the prayers of her children, I believe the Lord has a massive plan for you. When I said I could hear your heart beating yesterday... it was like I was hearing the heart of Jesus...in the piety chapel I prayed that one day Jesus would hug me so tightly that I could hear His heart and yesterday He answered that prayer."

I read this final text message from Eileen right before walking into the conference room for my meeting at St. Vincent Hospital. I had tears in my eyes as I walked into the room and someone immediately asked how I was doing. I simply responded, "I'm doing fantastic, because I had one of the best weekends of my life!" I could not stop praising God that morning!

I continued to pray harder and fast more to prepare myself for whatever the Lord may plan to show me in the future.

On June 1, 2023, three months after the CEW experiences that I had, I received a letter in the mail. Actually, it was two letters, and four pages of prayers. The two letters were handwritten – one from Valerie Martin and the other from Emily LeGreve. They both told me they had been praying and fasting for my intention since the women's CEW in March, to "help relieve my burden as Father Raj prompted me to pray and fast in preparation for more visions." They said they had been praying an "Act of Consecration to the Holy Spirit," had been asking for the intercession of St. John Bosco, and had been praying a "Litany for Holy Communion," all for my benefit, so that I continue to experience and witness to Jesus's true and Holy presence in the Blessed Sacrament!

Their letters and prayers moved me to tears as I read them. I also began praying daily, the same prayers as Valerie and Emily are praying for me each day. I am overwhelmed by the blessings the Lord has poured out on me, and the amazing faith-filled people and community that the Lord has surrounded me with. I am truly blessed!

Bear one another's burdens, and so you will fulfill the law of Christ. (1 Galtians 6:2)

Reflection questions:

In what ways have you borne another's burden in your life?

Have you ever asked God to relieve another person's burden, and place that burden on you instead? What were the circumstances that brought you to that prayer?

Are you in need of becoming more caring, compassionate, merciful, and empathetic to those in need?

Prayer:

Lord Jesus, Through your most precious body and blood, found and experienced in the Eucharist, may I grow more open each day to sharing in the burdens of your people. Provide me with the grace to grow each day in compassion, empathy, mercy, and love for my brothers and sisters in this world. Help me to be another Christ to those who are hurting, and suffering, and make you, Lord Jesus, more present to them in their lives. I ask this in your most Holy Name.

Amen.

A Spiritual Gift

CHAPTER 23

A Spiritual Gift

As I had mentioned in an earlier chapter, during the fall of 2015, a group of CEW members began meeting each Wednesday morning at 5 a.m. for an hour of Eucharistic Adoration followed by an hour and a half of bible study. This Adoration/Bible study group has continued to meet each week since. What began as a group of nine people gathering has now increased to consistently include more than 20 people attending each week.

On Wednesday morning, June 21, 2023, we were gathered in church for Eucharistic Adoration. About 15 minutes into Adoration, Jim Gillis, who typically sits toward the back of church, walked up to the front of church where I was, tapped me on the shoulder and said softly, "Mark is really struggling. We should all go and pray over him".

As a side note, this is not the first time Jim has made such a request during Adoration. Jim has a very special gift of being able to see, or read, things in people that most of us don't see or recognize. Because of this, although I had no idea what was going on with Mark, I got up to walk back to where Mark was sitting, which was about halfway back in church. Jim and I asked those at Adoration to come to where we were and pray over Mark.

Everyone in church for Eucharistic Adoration walked over to Mark, gathered around him, and laid our hands on him. Jim Gillis began praying out loud over Mark. After about 30 seconds of praying over Mark, Jim hesitated a second and then began praying in tongues.

As Jim began praying in tongues, I just quietly whispered, "Come Holy Spirit, come Holy Spirit," over and over, since I didn't know what Jim was praying.

As I continued to pray, "Come Holy Spirit," something amazing began happening! Although Jim was still praying in tongues, I suddenly was able to understand what he was praying! Jim kept repeating two separate phrases. "Mother Mary, come and be with him. God our Father, come be with him and bless him." Jim repeated these two phrases at least five times that I could understand.

As Jim continued to pray, this amazing sense of peace overcame me. I began tearing up, as I could feel the presence of the Holy Spirit encircling us. Mark was also weeping as we continued to lay hands on him as Jim prayed.

Following Adoration, we went as a group to the parish

hall in the basement of the church for Bible study. I was so overwhelmed by the experience of having understood what Jim had been praying, that I had to share it with our bible study group. Jim Gillis was also amazed because he had no idea what he was praying.

I have been told of people being blessed with the spiritual gift to interpret tongues, but have never actually experienced someone interpreting tongues. I have been present on a number of occasions when someone has prayed in tongues, but had never before been able to understand what they were saying while praying in tongues.

I spoke to my spiritual director, Monsignor Jim Feely about having been able to understand what Jim Gillis had been praying. Father Jim told me that he has presided at Masses for the Charismatic Movement in our Diocese and has witnessed people praying in tongues and others interpreting tongues, but he, himself, hasn't been blessed with those gifts. Although I already knew it, he told me what a blessing it was that I was given that experience.

Since this was the only time this had ever happened to me, Father Jim said that I may need to experience someone else praying in tongues to find out if I have been given a permanent gift of interpreting tongues or if it was a one-time occurrence. I'm waiting in anticipation to experience someone else praying in tongues in my presence to find out if I have been given a permanent gift!

> *There are different kinds of spiritual gifts but the same Spirit; there are different forms of service but the same Lord; there are different workings but the same God who produces all of them in everyone. To each individual the manifestation of the Spirit is given for some benefit.*

> *To one is given through the Spirit the expression of wisdom; to another the expression of knowledge according to the same Spirit; to another faith by the same Spirit; to another gifts of healing by the one Spirit; to another mighty deeds; to another prophecy; to another discernment of spirits: to another varieties of tongues; to another interpretation of tongues. But one and the same Spirit produces all of these, distributing them individually to each person as he wishes.*
> (1 Corinthians 12:4-11)

Reflection questions:

Have you witnessed any spiritual gifts manifested in others?

Has the Lord blessed you with any spiritual gifts that you are aware of?

If you have not received spiritual gifts, have you ever prayed for them?

Prayer:

Loving and gracious God, giver of all good gifts, I open my heart and ask this of you. If it be your desire, grace me with Spiritual gifts that you desire me to have. Through these gifts, use me as your instrument to bear witness to Your true and holy presence in my life and in the world. I ask this through Jesus Christ our Lord.

Amen.

Nothing Greater or Holier

CHAPTER 24

Nothing Greater or Holier

As I have gone out to parishes and shared my witness, in particular when sharing it with middle and high school students, I always ask if anyone thinks Mass is boring. Inevitably, the majority of the students will raise their hands. I obviously ask this question, knowing what the response will be. If you press the students as to why the Mass is boring, it usually comes down to just a couple of things. First, they can't relate to the music or the preaching, and second, they don't understand what is going on at Mass.

My response is always the same. If you are bored at Mass, what is it that you bring to the Mass? We shouldn't be going to Mass to be entertained. It shouldn't be all about what we get from Mass (although this is extremely important too), but rather what we give. As God reminded me during noon Mass at St. Willebrord's on that Monday in February of 2018, we come to Mass to worship and praise the Son of God, the Lamb of God. We are meant to give – to give our worship and praise to our God, to offer thanksgiving to the LORD, to give our very selves to Him! In return, Jesus gives His very self to us, in the Eucharist! The greatest self-giving gift we will ever receive!

As Bishop David Ricken stated in his Pastoral Letter, *Jesus in the Eucharist – Disciples Called to Worship*, "The Mass is not entertainment, it is a drama, divine drama that does not entertain but mystically moves us deeper into the reality of the Lord's self-giving sacrifice offered to the Father for the salvation of all mankind; each and every person and each and every age of human history."

If that does not get us excited, what will? Shouldn't the bread and wine being consecrated at Mass – being changed into the very body and blood of Jesus Christ, for us to consume – be the most exciting thing that we can ever participate in? And if so, how can that possibly be boring? We can never get so intimately close to Jesus and to heaven than when we participate in the Mass!

When explained this way, the reactions I get back from students are agreement that maybe the Mass really isn't boring, that the Mass is something to be totally excited about participating in! Perhaps, we as adults need that same reminder on occasion.

I believe that the key thing to remember is we need

to approach the Mass with the correct disposition and an open heart. I know this can be difficult, as sometimes when attending Mass, we all can be distracted, by thoughts or worries, distracted by things other than what is taking place right before our eyes on the altar.

Because I know I am far from being a perfect Christian, I too struggle with being fully attentive at Mass, struggle with temptations and sinfulness just like everyone else, I have often wondered, why has God allowed me to see and experience the things that I have in the presence of the Blessed Sacrament? I really don't know, but I have to believe that it might be that I do my best to come before the Lord in the Blessed Sacrament with an open heart, an open disposition, thus allowing the Holy Spirit to open my eyes, to pull back the veil to expose hidden sacred realities.

These experiences, seeing these hidden realities, have completely changed me. They have made my prayer life much deeper and more meaningful, which has made my relationship with the God much stronger, and in turn has made me much more dependent on God.

God has revealed to me that what St. Peter Julian Eymard said in his book, In the Light of the Monstrance, is absolutely true, "There is nothing greater or holier that we can do on earth than (spend time in) Eucharistic

Adoration." However, I would probably add to that statement, paraphrasing it in this way, "There is nothing greater or holier that we can do on earth than to spend time with Jesus in Eucharistic Adoration and in receiving Him in the Holy Eucharist at Mass."

To adore Jesus in the Blessed Sacrament is to share in the lives of the angels and saints in heaven, who never stop praising, blessing, and adoring Jesus, the Lamb of God. Because Jesus is the Eucharist, grace pours forth from the Eucharist. There is no greater grace to be found than in Jesus in the Eucharist, and in the Eucharist we find the ultimate gift of love.

As Saint Mother Teresa of Calcutta had said, "When you look at the crucifix, you understand how much Jesus loved you then. When you look at the Sacred Host, you understand how much Jesus loves us now."

I was given a Blessed Carlo Acutis prayer card by my friend Jim Gillis. Blessed Carlo was a Catholic Italian teenager who died in 2006 at the age of 15 of fulminant leukemia. After receiving his First Communion at the age of 7, Carlo began attending daily Mass. He had a deep devotion to the Blessed Sacrament and to the Blessed Mother, praying the Rosary daily. He was considered by many to be a computer genius and developed a website chronicling

Eucharistic Miracles from around the world. Carlo was beatified on Oct. 10, 2020.

On the prayer card that Jim had given me is this quote from Carlo, "The more we receive the Eucharist, the more we will become like Jesus, so that on this earth we will have a foretaste of heaven." I pray these words every day as part of my morning prayers. When praying this quote, I am always brought back to the words of Father Mark Mleziva, after I saw the tornado of angels gather around the altar during Benediction on Feb. 25, 2018, "Every once in a while, God will pull back the veil just a tiny bit and give us a little glimpse of heaven."

My prayer for each of us is this: That we can open our hearts, even just a crack, to allow the Holy Spirit to enter in and fill us to overflowing. That we will have a deep desire and longing to receive Jesus in the Eucharist. That we have the open disposition to see with eyes of faith when God chooses to pull back the veil, just a little bit, so we can all experience heaven on earth, and I pray that the Body and Blood of our Lord Jesus Christ brings us all to everlasting life. Amen!

Betsy's and my wedding, June 17, 1989 – Lighting the Unity Candle. St. Mary's Catholic Church, Tisch Mills, WI.

The wine decanter I saw blood running down the inside of during Mass at All Saints Parish, Denmark, WI.

The "Face of Jesus" in the curtain behind the tabernacle,
February 2019. All Saints Church, Denmark, WI.

Invocation of the Holy Spirit/Laying on of Hands
Diaconate Ordination Mass, May 19, 2012.
St. Francis Xavier Cathedral, Green Bay, WI.

Lying prostrate during the Litany of Saints
Diaconate Ordination Mass, May 19, 2012. Me on the far right.
St. Francis Xavier Cathedral, Green Bay, WI.

Bishop Ricken and me, immediately following the Diaconate
Ordination Mass, May 19, 2012.
St. Francis Xavier Cathedral, Green Bay, WI.

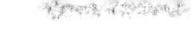

My family following my Ordination – Betsy, me, Grace, and John
St. Francis Xavier Cathedral, Green Bay, WI.

Mike Reel and Me following my Ordination – May, 19, 2012
St. Francis Xavier Cathedral, Green Bay, WI.

My first Mass serving as deacon, with Father Ron Colombo.
4:00 PM Mass, Saturday, May 19, 2012.
All Saints Catholic Church, Denmark, WI.

Christian Experience Weekend Eucharistic Adoration Chapel.
All Saints Catholic Church, Denmark, WI.

My family together at Lava Lake, Big Sky, MT – August 2017.
Me, Grace, Betsy, and John.

My Family in Big Sky, MT – August 2020.
Grace, Betsy, John, and me.

Sources and References

Introduction

"…nearly seven-in-ten Catholics…" (http://www.pewresearch.org/fact-tank/2019/08/05/transubstantiation-eucharist-u-s-catholics/)

Chapter 5 - The Tornado

"When Mass is being celebrated…" (http://www.catholictradition.org/Angels/angels13b.htm) and (Saints' Quotes on Jesus in The Eucharist - Catholic Stand)

"One day when I…" (http://www.catholictradition.org/Angels/angels13b.htm)

"St. Gertrude had spoken about…"(http://www.catholictradition.org/Angels/angels13b.htm)

"The angels surround …" 13 Saint Quotes that Reveal the Mystical Nature of the Mass - (churchpop.com)

"The heavens open…" 13 Saint Quotes that Reveal the Mystical Nature of the Mass - (churchpop.com)

"They were laughing as if…" (Saints' Quotes on Jesus in The Eucharist - Catholic Stand)

"Are we the only ones…" The Saints & Their Eucharistic Encounters With Angels (catholicexchange.com)

"While I was saying Mass…"A Catholic Mom in Hawaii: Saintly Quotes - Angels and the Holy Mass (hicatholicmom.blogspot.com)

On the purpose of Angels, quoting The Catechism of the Catholic Church, "The existence of the spiritual, non-corporeal beings that Sacred Scripture usually calls "angels" is a truth of faith.

- 335 In her liturgy, the Church joins with the angels to adore the thrice-holy God.
- 350 Angels are spiritual creatures who glorify God without ceasing.
- 351 The Angels surround Christ their Lord. They serve Him especially in the accomplishment of His saving mission to men."

Catechism_of_the_Catholic_Church_On_Angels.pdf (d2y1pz2y630308.cloudfront.net)

On the doctrine of the Church of an angles purpose see; (www.catholic365.com/article/2043/the-catholic-teaching-on-angels-part-1-the-angles.hmtl The Catholic Teachings On The Angels - Part 1: The Angels (catholic365.com))

Chapter 6 - *The Lamb's Supper*

"At Mass, we are not alone…
(https://etcatholic.org/2013/10/scott-hahn-jesus-says-what-he-means-means-what-he-says/)

Chapter 10 - *Blessed by Jesus*

"Prayer for Eucharistic Adoration:
I adore You, Bread from Heaven…"
Prayers For Eucharistic Adoration - Powerful & Uplifting Words For Prayer (prayerist.com)

Chapter 13 - *The Weight of the Sins of the World*

St. Christopher Prayer:
St Christopher Prayer | DAILY PRAYERS (daily-prayers.org)

Chapter 15 - *You've Got to Carry That Weight*

The Way of the Cross… "As the strength of Jesus fails…"
The Way of the Cross (The Stations of the Cross) (lordcalls.com)

Prayer:
"O Lord Jesus, may it be our privilege to bear our cross…"
The Way of the Cross (The Stations of the Cross) (lordcalls.com)

Chapter 22 - *Nothing Greater or Holier*

"There is nothing greater or holier…" (St. Peter Julian Eymard, *In the Light of the Monstrance,* Page 177, Chapter V – Adoration of the Most Blessed Sacrament)

"When we look at the crucifix…" St. Francis Perpetual Eucharistic Adoration in Traverse City, MI (stfrancisadoration.org) - Blessed Mother Teresa Of Calcutta (1910 to 1997) - Quotes On The Importance Of Eucharistic Adoration

Made in the USA
Monee, IL
31 October 2023